Let Us Fight For Africa

Copyright 2007 Desmond Dudwa Phiri

All rights reserved. No part of this publication may be reproduced stored in a retrieval system, or transmitted in any form or by any means, electronic, mechanic, photocopying, recording or otherwise, without prior permission from the publishers.

Published by
Kachere Series
P.O. Box 1037, Zomba, Malawi
ISBN 978-99908-87-03-7

Represented outside Africa by
African Books Collective, Oxford (orders@africanbookscollective.com)
Michigan State University Press, East Lansing (msupress@msu.edu)

Layout: Josephine Kawejere.
Cover Design: Caroline Chihana

Printed by Lightning Source

Let Us Fight For Africa

A Play based on the John Chilembwe Rising of 1915

Desmond Dudwa Phiri

Kachere Books no. 31

Kachere Series
Zomba
2007

Kachere Series,
P.O. Box 1037,
Zomba, Malawi
kachere@globemw.net
www.sdnp.org.mw/kachereseries/

This book is part of the Kachere Series, a range of books on religion, culture and society in Malawi. Related titles are

Patrick Makondesa, *Moyo ndi Utumiki wa Mbusa ndi Mai Muocha wa Providence Industrial Mission.*

Patrick Makondesa, *The Church History of Providence Industrial Mission.*

George Shepperson and Tom Price, *Independent African. John Chilembwe and the Nyasaland rising of 1915.*

Harry Langworthy, *Africa for the African. The Life of Joseph Booth.*

Klaus Fiedler, *The Making of a Maverick Missionary. Joseph Booth in Australasia.*

Hubert Reijnaerts, Ann Nielsen and Matthew Schoffeleers, *Montfortians in Malawi. Their Spirituality and their Missionary Approach.*

Andrew C. Ross, *Blantyre Mission and the Making of Modern Malawi.*

James Tengatenga, *Church, State and Society in Malawi. The Anglican Case.*

John McCracken, *Politics & Christianity in Malawi 1875-194. The Impact of the Livingstonia Mission in the Northern Province.*

The Kachere Series is the publications arm of the Department of Theology and Religious Studies of the University of Malawi

Series Editors: J.C. Chakanza, F.L. Chingota, Klaus Fiedler, P.A. Kalilombe, Chimwemwe Katumbi, Martin Ott, Imran Shareef Mahomed and F. Nsengiyumva

Let Us Fight For Africa

This is a historical play of the 1915 Nyasaland African uprising led by John Chilembwe.

In 1897 a freelance English missionary called Joseph Booth took with him to America his servant called John Chilembwe and handed him to American blacks who gave him a three year theological education. He returned in 1900 and founded his own church and school, wrote in the *Nyasaland Times* he was to make an African a worthy member of the human race and indomitable.

In the course of time thousands of Africans visited Chilembwe to complain about the manner they were being treated as tenants and workers on European estates. Some complained of how they were being rounded up for taxes or conscripted for military services. The Government ordered Chilembwe not to build any more schools. He saw the government, the business community and some of the missionaries as hostile to Africans.

On 23rd January, 1915 he led 1000 men in a rising to drive out foreign rulers of the country and set up a government of his own. The rising was crushed within two weeks. His death was kept a mystery for several decades. Many of his followers believed he has escaped to America via Scotland.

In 1958 Professor George Shepperson of Edinburgh University published a biography of John Chilembwe titled *Independent African* which has become a source book for African studies in Africa and abroad. This book has contributed to the popularity of Chilembwe's name among students of African history and the public in general.

In 1994, January 15 was declared a public holiday in Malawi in memory of Chilembwe. The Malawi currency now is imprinted with Chilembwe's portrait. Plays are aired on the radio and TV both on Chilembwe Day and Martyr's day (March 3).

The author of this play has also written a biography of John Chilembwe called *Let us Die for Africa* which contains material not found in Shepperson's book. This play has been written in response to public demand for a genuine play on which they would like to base their annual recordings.

As Chilembwe's name is now revered throughout Africa, the play is likely to be of continental interest.

The author has written sixteen other books covering history, biographies, a novel and a play published by Evans Brothers of London in 1968 which has ever since been used in schools in Africa and America. Until recently it was on the syllabus of schools in Botswana.

Let Us Fight For Africa

Act One

Scene I

At Magomero, Bruce Estates

Characters:
Wilson Zimba, Foreman
Bvomera Zonse, Assistant Foreman
Kondani, A thangata *(labour rent) tenant*
M'maniwa, A thangata *(labour rent) tenant*
Nzima, A worker for tax money
Morrison, Chilembwe's nephew

(The time is midday, tenants and workers have been working since sunrise. Now they are thirsty and hungry. Zimba the foreman has been away at the Providence Industrial Mission attending Chilembwe's meeting, leaving the workers under Bvomera Zonse, his assistant).

Workers singing as they work

From sunrise to sunset,
We toil without rest.
From dawn to dusk,
Hungry and thirsty we work.
Oh, what sort of master is this we have!
He does not care that we starve.

Bvomera Zonse *(clapping hands angrily)*
Hey, you people there, stop that foolish song.
Every word you utter is wrong.
Mr. Livingstone Bruce is a kind-hearted landlord,

He is nice to all, the young and the old.
You dwell on his land from January to December,
But *thangata* work you do only three months, September, October, November.
You say you toil from sunrise to sunset.
Well, that's only half a day, do not forget.
Sing nicely or do not sing at all,
Otherwise with my boots I kick you like a ball.

Kondani   We sing like this,
                  Hoping that you as one of us,
                  Will plead with our master
                  To treat us better.

M'maniwa   Have you not heard that hunger
                  Kindles in a man fierce anger?
                  Give us food
                  We will then sing a song that's good.

Bvomera Zonse Shame on you for what you have said,
                  Are you talking to the foreman or a maid?
                  I have orders to flog
                  He that croaks like a frog. *(lashes Nzima)*

Nzima   Why do you flog me?

Bvomera Zonse Be working harder,
                  Do not just stand there.
                  If I tell the master that you are lazy, he will evict you from this land.

Nzima   I am not a tenant on Bruce's land,
                  I have enough soil of my own in Ngoniland.
                  While I was taming bees for honey
                  The Resident Magistrate demanded from me tax money.
                  Since I did not have any
                  The resident forced me to leave
                  My dear home for Bruce Estate
                  Where I do work that I hate.
                  For one year I have toiled,
                  But I am paid like a child.

Bvomera Zonse	Too much you have bubbled, now shut up,
	Else I knock your teeth till down they drop,
	(Turning round and facing others)
	What I say to him, is meant for you all,
	Work hard and work always at my beck and call.
Kondani	In the manner you abuse us
	One would think we are a pack of asses,
	Do not forget we are like you,
	We are black and you are black too.
	Have pity on us your fellow natives
	Who toil for hire like slaves
	On land God gave our ancestors,
	Which the planters and the chiefs dispossessed us.
Bvomera Zonse	Kondani, do no not waste the day,
	It's all rubbish what you say.
	Loyalty I first give to Mr. Bruce,
	Next to the Manager Mr. Livingstone, Jarvis.
	They pay me a fair salary every month,
	This buys food for my stomach and mouth.
	Indeed, for my wives and children too,
	I do not care what happens to you
	So longs as Mr. Bruce increases my salary
	To him my loyalty grows day by day.
	(Still chasing and flogging workers, enters Wilson Zimba)
Wilson Zimba	*(Arriving smartly dressed)* Bvomera Zonse, why do you treat workers like that?
	Shouting at them, flogging them, for what?
	Has your heart hardened like a stone,
	Treating our people like Jarvis Livingstone?
Bvomera Zonse	Nothing is wrong with the way I treat the workers,
	I am just fulfilling our masters orders.
	Of course Zimba you are my boss too,
	But my salary comes from the Whiteman
	Not from you my fellow Blackman.
	To me nothing else matters
	But the approval of Bruce and Livingstone my white masters

Zimba	Don't you fear the owner of these men?
Bvomera Zonse	That question I don't understand; In it seems there is something underhand.
Zimba	Underhand, why do you say that?
Zonse	This much I understand, He that owns the land Owns all things found thereon The soil, crops, animals and the men.
Zimba	These people don't belong to Bruce, the landlord, They belong to the Creator, Almighty God, And God has appointed as His overseer Pastor John Chilembwe Who baptizes men and women in the River Mbombwe. We must treat the workers as justly as Chilembwe says; For his people's freedom daily he prays.
Zonse	Zimba, if I had not known you before I would have called you a mere bore. All these years you have been thundering commands With all these workers to please our masters, Now you countermand our masters' orders; why? Speak the truth, don't lie.
Zimba	It is true in the past I carried out All orders from Bruce and Livingstone without Caring how much misery and pain On my fellow Africans I inflicted just to gain More money, promotion and praise. I swore at the wretched people those days, But now I am a follower of John Chilembwe. Since the day he baptized me in the River Mbombwe. Chilembwe says we should be proud of our race, And that to ill-treat fellow Africans is a disgrace. Therefore Zonse I command you to Stop abusing fellow blacks, no matter what they do.
Bvomera Zonse	If you are tired of money, Zimba, Go back home, whether Chintheche or Mzimba. But do not try to instill

	In me foolish ideas against my will. *(Turning towards the people)* Get on working you bloody people. I command you, in the name of Livingstone Bruce the noble.
Zimba	Do not listen to Zonse, oh people of God, His dignity for money he has sold, He loves not his fellow blacks but money. I have a message for you that is sweeter than honey, The message from Chilembwe the Chosen one of God, He is to us what Moses was to the Hebrews in the days of old. To the toilers Moses brought food and rest, So will Chilembwe do to his people that which is best. Come near me all of you. Don't leave women and children behind, Chilembwe loves them too.
Kondani	Fellow toilers down your tools, be quick, Walking slowly, why has hunger made you even sick?
Zimba	Last night I went to the Providence Industrial Mission, By the River Mbombwe is where you find this Mission Station, There I found gathered well-attired and dignified women, For yesterday was a holy Sunday, But today is a blue Monday. Chilembwe gazed at me sternly: 'Tell me, Zimba', he said firmly, Is it true that you there at Magomero Estate Abuse our fellow Africans using words in bad taste? And make them toil from early morning To very late evening Without a moment of rest?" Having said this he stared at me unblinking. I did not know what he was thinking, All the same I gathered courage, And said "Pastor, I am a man in bondage By my master, I am commanded to do anything good or bad.

Of course this is sad,
But under the *thangata* system things are such
That, if we do not please our masters very much,
They flog or evict us,
And there is no one to give us redress."
Some people preach Christianity,
But they practise cruelty.
Not so Chilembwe, you may ask how.
However, let me not speak too much for now,
One of you, go behind that anthill,
Say to the people you find there, Zimba says come, and they will.
(A procession of women and men with baskets and pots, singing)
We are bringing you food from John Chilembwe,
The man who baptized us in the River Mbombwe.
He has heard you toil without rest or food,
What your masters do to you is not good.

>Bringing you the food,
>Bringing you the food,
>We come rejoicing with baskets full.
>Bringing you the food,
>Bringing you the food,
>From John Chilembwe our leader, merciful.

Kondani   What a procession!
Will there
Be a wedding feast?

Zimba   Wait and see.

M'maniwa   Who is that at the head of the procession,
Jumping as he sings in front of everyone?

Zimba   That is Morrison,
Though he is Chimpele's son
He is more devoted to Chilembwe, his uncle.
(The procession arrives)

Zimba   Open the baskets so that they may see
The banquet such as Christ gave to the people of Galilee.

Kondani	Ah! *Nsima* with beans all red, On top pieces and pieces of bread. What a day this is today, M'maniwa, what do you say?
M'maniwa	Here I have *nsima* with *chambo* fish Contained in a beautiful dish.
Nzima	Never have I eaten food so tasty. The women who cooked this food were not hasty, They did the job with great care and skill, The flour they used must have come from a special mill, Honourable guest, is there a school where women learn to cook better? If so allow us to send our wives there.
Morrison	Thank you for the nice words you have said about this food, I will go and tell the women who cooked it; they will feel good. All women who participated in cooking these dishes Have undergone instruction under Mrs. Ida Chilembwe, my uncle's wife of course. She herself was taught by Emma DeLany, Miss. All of you bring your wives To my aunt; teaching others is what she likes.
Kondani	Why does the great teacher not open a school here At Magomero; to us all, such a school will be near?
Morrison	Blame not Chilembwe but your boss Livingstone. That man has a heart as hard as a stone. He has refused us permission while using his abusive words To let Chilembwe build here a school or a prayer house. Between the two men the future Looks bleak, of this I am sure.
Nzima	Allow me, Sir, before you depart To recite a poetic song of thanks set apart For doers of great things, Suitable for Chilembwe a man of compassion and kindness.

Morrison	Go ahead, let us hear the song, To stop a man saying thanks is wrong.
Nzima	Praise be to Chilembwe, friend of the helpless, Chilembwe, father to all of us, He heard we were starving. Chilembwe cares for us all his people. Today we have feasted as if at the wedding of a noble. Let us acclaim Chilembwe and shout *bayete*. Shout loud enough for people to hear as far as Tete.
Morrison	Next Sunday there will be a congregation At the Providence Industrial Mission, People will come from near and far, Come and let me introduce you to our master. My uncle Chilembwe will be glad to see you. Not only you the poet but all of you, For Chilembwe does not say you and you come, To everyone without distinction he says "welcome."
Nzima	Thank you for the invitation. Next Sunday you will see us all at the Providence Industrial Mission. *(Morrison departs)*
Wilson Zimba	Eat and finish the food, Then resume working in thirty minutes time Chilembwe must not be misunderstood To encourage idleness, it is a crime *(Wilson Zimba departs)*

Scene II

Livingstone, Zonse, Zimba, Chimbiya, M'maniwa, Nzima, Linjesi, women and children

(Livingstone arrives carrying a chikoti, *a hippo-skin whip, wearing a tunic and helmet, finds the workers singing and dancing.)*

Livingstone	Zonse, what are these people doing here? Who authorized you or anybody to give them beer?

Bvomera Zonse	Sir, what these people are doing Is indeed most disgusting, But Sir do not blame me. Instead blame the man you promoted above me as a senior supervisor, Zimba and no other person. Sir, Zimba has come to work this morning simply to order Your tenants and workers to sit down, carouse and not bother To listen to what I order them to do, But to heed only John Chilembwe, The Black Pastor with a school of his own by the River Mbombwe.
Livingstone	Has Zimba become mad?
Zonse	Sir, I don't know, but what he has done is indeed very bad.
Livingstone	Where is he? Fetch him.
Zonse	He has gone this way with Morrison *(Zonse shouts for Zimba)*. The boss is here. He wants you at once. Zimba arrives hands in pocket
Livingstone	Come on, be quick boy, When I call you come running.
Zimba	My walking is speedy enough.
Livingstone	Rubbish! And how dare you order my workers to loaf around and rest At midday; carouse and dance with zest.
Zimba	He told me that subjects of the king in England Work shorter hours there than we do here in Nyasaland. In Britain workers work and then have a break During which they have snacks that include a cake. He said here at Magomero estate we blacks, Whether as tenants or workers are treated like slaves From 6 am to 6 pm we toil without rest, Are paid little for doing a lot,

	This is not *thangata* at all,
	He says, but slavery, physical and mental.
Livingstone	Who is this bastard you refer to as he, he?
Zimba	He is not a bastard, I must correct that, Sir.
	He is a homegrown missionary, teacher and pastor.
	I am talking of John Chilembwe, the man chosen by God
	To lead us blacks. He is kind hearted, religious and bold.
	Having revealed his name, may
	I recount what else Chilembwe said on 23 May?
Livingstone	What else did the bloody native say?
Zimba	Chilembwe has sent this food to us, his people,
	Hoping you will follow the good example
	And treat us likewise from tomorrow
	All over the Bruce Estates beginning at Magomero.
Livingstone	Tell the bloody native Chilembwe, if he continues
	Poking his broad and flat nose
	Into the vast Bruce Estates,
	I will break him into pieces.
	Whatever he takes himself to be,
	To me he is like an ape dwelling in a tree
Zimba	I dare not go and repeat that.
Livingstone	Why not?
Zimba	Like you he is a man with short temper.
Livingstone	How Chilembwe responds I don't care,
	He must no more dare,
	To interrupt a day's work at Magomero,
	Right from today, not tomorrow.
	And you must stop at once
	Being a follower of the bloody fool or else-
Zimba	Bloody fool, Let us correct that,
	Neither I nor Chilembwe deserves the insult.
Livingstone	Tell me, Wilson, why so many of you natives
	Flock to Chilembwe's home and get turned into knaves.

	I remember once to have seen him, he hardly looked five feet tall.
	Unlike me he is not a personality at all.
	Is he not fooling you with his magic?
	And some other trick?
Zimba	Chilembwe does not know any kind of magic,
	Neither does he use any trick.
	He commands the respect of us all
	Africans for more reasons than I can recall.
	He went to America and returned with BA and BD degrees
	He has an education no one can despise,
	But his high education alone
	Would not attract each and everyone,
	Chilembwe is a man from God,
	Which is more important than having gold.
	There in America he heard the voice of the Most High:
	"Go back home and lead your people like Moses descending from Mount Sinai."
Livingstone	This native Chilembwe is a bore,
	Do not associate with him anymore.
	His subversive activities will cost you dear,
	This I must make to you very clear.
Zimba	What you say, Sir, is hard to bear.
	When my friends go to Chilembwe,
	Why should I not also be there?
Zonse	If to you Chilembwe is good, then
	Depart; don't remain to spoil us fellow workers here as if we were your children.
Zimba	Zonse, you are talking that nonsense
	Because you walk in darkness.
	Know this, Christ our Spiritual Saviour,
	Has appointed Chilembwe the black people's earthly leader.
Livingstone	Enough of that, I dismiss you,
	Quit this place and immediately too.
Zimba	Before I quit pay me my terminal benefits,
	I have been working here for thirteen years.

	You cannot just send me away empty handed,
	I will be financially stranded.
Livingstone	Go, go quickly you bastard.
	You deserve no gratuity of any kind.
Zimba	If you do not pay me my gratuities, I'll go and see Mr. Mitchell,
	The Resident Magistrate and tell
	Him that here at Magomero
	Africans are oppressed. I will go right tomorrow.
Livingstone	You may as well go to the *boma* now
	And tell Mitchell what else I have also done to you.
	(Livingstone whips Zimba)
Zimba	Oh, you can't do that to me,
	Today you will see.
	(Zimba removes his coat ready to fight)
Zonse	Eh, eh Zimba, don't dare
	Fight our white master.
	(Pushes Zimba)
Livingstone	Let the brute dare
	Touch me; with this revolver
	I will blow off his baboon like head
	And he will roll down there dead.
	(Zimba flees upon seeing the revolver)
Livingstone	Now that I have fired Wilson,
	As the new supervisor you carry on.
Zonse	Thank you Sir for making me a supervisor,
	But my work may still be disturbed because
	Of three remaining die-hard Chilembwe men,
	They are very stubborn.
Livingstone	Go and summon the bastards.
Zonse	*Shouts* Chimbiya, M'maniwa, Nzima - come running!
Zonse	Just see, Sir, I told them to come running,
	Instead they come walking.

	Sir, they do not fear you any more at all, But they say Chilembwe is the greatest of all.
Livingstone	*(Shouts)* Come on, be quick you bloody baboons! Don't waste my precious moments!
Chimbiya	We are human beings like you, If we are baboons then you are a baboon too.
Livingstone	How dare you say that to me, *(Flogs him)* I order you to quit Bruce's land!
Chimbiya	Why evict me from the land I inherited from my ancestors?
M'maniwa	Indeed, Sir, what has Chimbiya done to deserve this?
Livingstone	You also quit the land, pack up and go, Today not tomorrow! *(flogs him)*
Nzima	I am not working for tenancy. Give me my wages, I too will be glad to quit This estate of slavery.
Livingstone	No, just quit and quickly too. *(Flogs them again. Chimbiya, M'maniwa, Nzima confer)*
Linjesi	Sir, two gentlemen have arrived at your house.
Livingstone	Do you know who they are?
Linjesi	I don't know them, to be frank, But one is white and the other one is black.
Livingstone	In that case there is only one gentleman Accompanied by a native man. Do not misuse the word gentlemen, It applies only to white men. *(Turning to Zonse)* I am going to see what business the gentleman has with me Make sure each of your men is as busy as a bee.
Zonse	I will do as you command, Sir.

Scene III

Livingstone, Rev. Hetherwick, Moffat, Kanchanda, Eric Wilberforce, Rev. and Mrs. Hollis, Linjesi

Livingstone	Good afternoon, Rev. Hetherwick.
Hetherwick	Good afternoon, Mr. Livingstone.
Livingstone	I hope I have not kept you waiting for too long In the course of putting right things done wrong here. It's not in keeping with our tradition in Scotland To treat a fellow Scotsman with discourtesy in Nyasaland.
Hetherwick	You haven't kept us waiting. To the contrary, thank you for sparing Your time to come and attend to us Though we arrived without giving you advance notice.
Livingstone	May I introduce to you this young gentleman Born and brought up in the Isle of Man. He is Eric Wilberforce, He has come to assist me and Mr. Bruce.
Hetherwick	Good afternoon, Mr. Wilberforce.
Wilberforce	Good afternoon, Reverend.
Hetherwick	May I also introduce to you the gentleman you see standing there; He is Mr. Moffat Kanchanda, a teacher, and Church Elder.
Livingstone	You missionaries are spoiling the natives, what a pity. In your zeal to convert them to Christianity You make them think they are equals of whitemen By referring to them as gentlemen.
Hetherwick	But how do we address those natives who look more civilized than others? We at the mission cannot do otherwise but call them sisters and brothers.
Livingstone	All the time I prefer to remind the Native he is a savage. I am part of two thousand years of Christian civilization that

	Has grown from age to age.
	Those who slack I flog; the result
	Is that they work with zeal,
	Our harvest and profits amount to a good deal.
Hetherwick	You could get even better results
	Out of the native's labour
	If you treated him better than a mule.
	The pain you inflict on him, he will not for long endure.
Livingstone	Ah, wait a minute, Reverend,
	The means are justified by the end.
	While at every estate on the Shire Highlands planters suffer losses,
	Here at Magomero every year we realize profits.
Hetherwick	Sorry, Mr. Livingstone to interrupt you,
	We have digressed from the subject that has to do
	With our sudden visit which is to seek your permission
	For our Church of Scotland Mission
	To open a school here at your farmland
	As we have done elsewhere in Southern Nyasaland.
Livingstone	If the school is to be for
	European children, the request could be considered.
Hetherwick	It will be for African children.
Livingstone	I cannot allow a school
	For Natives here; I know better than to behave like a fool.
	Unless the school is under European Supervision,
	I am afraid, it will be spreading among our workers
	Chilembwe's activities of subversion.
Hetherwick	We are going to place the school under Moffat Kanchanda the Church elder,
	He is a civilized African, in habits very sober.
	He has caused us no trouble at the mission.
	He will cause you no trouble if you grant us the permission.
Livingstone	You are not getting my point, Reverend
	Moffat is a native, as such there is nothing about him to defend,

	At this farm we had a native foreman called Wilson who did his work well,
	But one day I discovered he was a prince of hell,
	He was spreading the subversive teachings of John Chilembwe,
	The pig-headed native Pastor by the River Mbombwe.
	Reverend, if you cannot provide a European master for the school,
	Drop the idea; anyway why bother educating the native, he is an incurable fool.
Hetherwick	Incurable fool, how can you say that, Mr. Livingstone;
	My experience with the native is a very happy one.
Livingstone	Let me be frank with you and your mission;
	What you teach natives in schools is open to suspicion.
	Most of the boys from your school refuse to take off their hats
	To a whiteman walking or standing nearby.
	If I order and command them to do so, they ask why.
	For white men they show no respect.
	Of all your school leavers Chilembwe I particularly detest.
Hetherwick	If we treat natives with justice
	And put our Christianity into practice,
	They will give us respect.
	For us at the Mission a native is a person to love not to detest.
	As to the taking off of hats by an African
	In the presence of a European,
	I give no ruling to the African.
	I have at times seen a native take off his hat, salute a European;
	The European has given no response
	As if what the native has done is nonsense.
	You know in Britain when a drummer boy gives a salute
	To General Kitchener, he responds with his own salute.
Livingstone	Go on, you have not said anything about the subversive John Chilembwe.

Hetherwick	It is true, Chilembwe attended our Chilomoni School when it was near the big tree. He left the school having passed standard three. Thereafter he fell into the hands of the eccentric Joseph Booth, From whom he imbibed falsehoods masquerading as truth.
Livingstone	You must now bear part of the blame, And even the shame, For all the troubles Chilembwe is causing At the Bruce Estates by inciting Our tenants and workers to indiscipline. It is high time Chilembwe was thrown into prison.
Hetherwick	Mainstream Christian missions Also have got misgivings about Chilembwe's intentions. He builds his schools too close in ours And receives into his Church those men We have suspended for indiscipline.
Livingstone	What then are you going to do Reverend, To put this nuisance to an end?
Hetherwick	We are trying by persuasions To bring him into the Federation of Christian Missions, Where we reaffirm at each annual conference To continue respecting each other's sphere of influence.
Livingstone	Why bring into your association A leopard to devour you from within? The best thing is to ask the Government To arrest Chilembwe and send him to banishment.
Hetherwick	Must we go as far as that?
Livingstone	Why not? Chilembwe is having bad influence On Our tenants' conscience, He is impacting evil influence. I have heard them shout 'Africa for Africans' and all that. This is what Chilembwe is teaching them. His mission has nothing to do with Jesus of Jerusalem.

Hetherwick	We of the Blantyre Mission have at times Talked of Africa for Africans, But not in the anti-European sense. Man's humanity to man is the substance Of what we teach and urge white people to accept The Blackman as a brother and treat him with due respect.
Livingstone	As a brother?
Hetherwick	But as what?
Livingstone	I am in agreement with the Boer When he says the Blackman is a hewer Of wood and drawer of water For the white man. This must be so everywhere under the sun.
Hetherwick	How can say such a thing Mr. Willie Livingstone So different from the humanity of your kinsman Dr. David Livingstone?
Livingstone	To hell with David Livingstone, a wanderer in search of rivers, My hero is Cecil John Rhodes. He came to Africa and amassed wealth, Which he used to found colonies before his untimely death. The colonies which perpetuate his name as Southern and Northern Rhodesia. Thanks to Rhodes we can now sing here "Rule Britannia'.
Hetherwick	I can see now We are unable to agree on how To live with the natives; sorry I have wasted your time, I better depart for my mission and home.
Livingstone	Indeed it is time we part, There is not much to agree about.
	(Hetherwick departs. He is followed by Wilberforce. At a distance they converse)
Wilberforce	Reverend, can I have a word with you?
Hetherwick	Of course, not just one word, even two.

Wilberforce	If there is an opening At the Blantyre Mission For someone like me to teach School subjects and to preach, Please consider taking me on.
Hetherwick	Why do you want to leave the Bruce estates? Of all the estate owners in Nyasaland they are the most prosperous. The pay their European staff generously, Though with their native workers I'm told they are niggardly.
Wilberforce	I cannot agree more with what you say, The Negroes here suffer injustice everyday. I know from my experience in the West Indies That the manner Mr. Livingstone treats Negroes Here, bodes ill for the Bruce Estates future. Negroes won't in silence forever endure The injustices, I see dark clouds gathering in the sky, I fear next there will be thunder, no wonder why.
Hetherwick	How delighted would I be to help you leave the city of destruction On a pilgrimage to the Celestial City by joining our Mission. Unfortunately, just now we cannot hire more staff The mission budget is not big enough, But I have taken note of your desire. I will remember you in my prayer. *(Exit Hetherwick and Wilberforce, enter Hollis and his wife)*
Linjesi	Are you going back, Sir? But I see another white man and his *donna* coming there.
Livingstone	*(Aside)* From the crumpled dress of the man And the shaggy hair of the woman I guess they are missionaries. Good morning, may I know who you are.
Hollis	Good morning Mr. Livingstone We are from the Church of the Saviour Mission.

	My name is John Hollis And this is my wife Doris.
Livingstone	You are another man of the Bible Teaching the natives how to cause us whites trouble.
Hollis	Not to cause trouble to anybody, But to make everyone feel they are somebody As they travel on the road to heaven, Not as whites or blacks but God's children.
Livingstone	I am sick of that stuff- What do you want from me? Answer in brief.
Hollis	Will you kindly sell us two sheep and two goats?
Livingstone	What for?
Hollis	We are to kill them to entertain our guests At the anniversary of our arrival here as Missionaries.
Livingstone	Who will be your guests?
Hollis	Mostly members of smaller churches.
Livingstone	Will you sit at the table with natives?
Hollis	Naturally, for we do not notice a person's colour. The Holy Spirit guides our behaviour.
Livingstone	Will you invite John Chilembwe to this feast?
Hollis	Naturally, our relationship with him is one of the best.
Livingstone	I have the goats and sheep, but not for sale to inferior whites like you.
Hollis	We may be inferior but we do God's work.
Livingstone	I have no business with those who allow natives to wear a hat and a tie While a white person is standing or passing nearby.
Hollis	What we do is to atone God for the white man's sin of enslaving the Blackman and taking him to America, By bringing the message of Christian charity and reconciliation to Africa.
Mrs. Hollis	Amen.

Livingstone	Go away, I command you. Don't waste my time, I have so much to do.

Scene IV

Livingstone, Bvomera Zonse, Wilberforce

	(The workers singing) Today is pay morning, For our thirty day's toiling We don't know what we shall get, But for sure, not enough to buy a packet of salt.
Bvomera Zonse	Shut up that song, The words you use are too strong For the ears of our good master. Sing a song that sounds better.
Livingstone	*(Sitting by the pay desk' with a bag full of coins)* Zonse read the first name on the payroll
Bvomera Zonse	*(Shouting)* Chipewa.
Chipewa	Yessah.
Bvomera Zonse	Come forward for your pay.
Chipewa	*(Gasps as he receives the money)* Why, Sir, only this Amount for working six to six All days of the month, This is not my labour's worth.
Livingstone	That's what your lazy hands are worth. Take it and shut up your mouth. *(Turning to Zonse)* Next!
Zonse	Johnstone Zilongolola
Zilongolola	*(Receiving the money)* Oh, no, boss, Four shillings for thirty days No, illiterates you may fool, But I have been to John Chilembwe's School,

	I can read and count. Give me the exact amount.
Livingstone	Go away before I spit into your face, You member of the accursed savage race.
Zilongolola	If you spit into my face, I too will spit into yours. If my race is savage, Yours is a heap of garbage.
Zonse	Zilongolola, you speak too much indeed. As your name suggests, How can you say that to a white man? *(Tries to push him off)*
Zilongolola	Don't touch me, you white man's dog Otherwise I knock you dead.
Livingstone	I thought you were going to push off The argumentative bastard. Why have you stopped?
Zonse	Sir, he has threatened me with death.
Livingstone	*(Rising from his seat)* Get Away from there you black ape. *(He lashes Zilongolola)*
Zilongolola	Like Wilson I am going straight To see the Resident Magistrate, The new one called Phillip Mitchell, And tell him you have turned Magomero into hell.
Livingstone	*(Pointing at men standing nearby)* You and you go there and seize the fool, The little education he acquired at Chilembwe's School I must purge out of him with twenty lashes. Your reward for bringing him back will be six shillings.

(Two men run after Zilongolola. Each pretends to fall down just to let Zilongolola escape)

Man 1	Sorry Sir, fast though we ran, We have failed to catch the man. As we ran each of us again and again

	Got entangled in a creeper and fell down.
Man 2	Sir, that man Zilongolola has magic; When I thought I had got hold of him by the neck, I found I was gripping a mere tree While he was at distance still free.
Livingstone	Whom do you mean to fool, you specimen of the savage race Good at nothing else but deceitfulness? For failing to catch the bastard and from me receive cash, I will now reward you with a lash. One on your lips. Another on your hips. *(Livingstone flogs them)*
Wilberforce	But why Mr. Livingstone? What wrong have these men done?
Livingstone	They have proved disloyal to me By failing to seize the native who has insulted me. *(Turning to foreman)* Next.
Zonse	Stand up! *(A girl stands up trembling)*
Livingstone	Here is a lot of money for you, three pence.
Wilberforce	The little girl has been drawing water, And looking after your daughter, For thirty days of the month. Give her her labour's worth.
Livingstone	What does the little monkey Know about the value of money?
Wilberforce	She must know the value of money, Otherwise why has she been working for it as a nanny?
Livingstone	I have a duty to keep Bruce Estates afloat, Free of heavy debts at any cost By not overpaying lazy natives.
Wilberforce	That a business must make a profit, I don't dispute that,

	But this does not mean That in paying natives we should be mean.
Livingstone	Wilberforce, you have been here six months net; Already you are proving insubordinate. It would be better for both of us If you tendered three month's notice, Resigned and went home to the Isle of Man. I would hate to sack a white man.
Wilberforce	Sooner or later you will have trouble With the natives, you keep them under conditions that are terrible. Allow me to give a shorter notice And find work where natives are treated with justice.
Livingstone	To that I won't say no. Right away you may pack up and go.

Act Two

Scene I

Complainants and petitioners at the Resident Magistrate's Office

Characters: Zimba, Phillip Mitchell, Chimbiya, Sagawa (Dumpling), Zione, Zione's grandmother

Mitchell	Mafuta!
Sagawa	Yessah. *(comes running)*
Mitchell	I see a crowd of people outside. They seem to be keen to come inside. Ask them what they have come for, And tell them not to stand near the door.
Sagawa	What you command, Sir, that will I do. But Sir, may I ask a simple favour of you?

Mitchell	Go ahead, Don't be afraid.
Sagawa	When people hear you call me Mafuta they laugh, The name Mafuta means Fatty to them this is funny enough. But I do not take kindly to their laughter, Please call me by the name your predecessor gave me, it sounds better.
Mitchell	What name did he give you?
Sagawa	He gave me the name Dumpling.
Mitchell	*(aside)* Poor fellow, he does not know that Fatty and Dumpling mean the same thing. Why do you like the name Dumpling?
Sagawa	It reminds me of my wife I address as darling.
Mitchell	I am willing to call you by your favourite name. Meanwhile I wonder what those people want - go and ask them. *(Dumpling goes and then comes back)*
Sagawa	Most of those people have come from the estate of Bruce Whose manager is Livingstone Jarvis. They ask if they may come and see what you can do With their complaints against Mr. Livingstone and Mr. Bruce too.
Mitchell	Since my clerk interpreter Somba Is not here having gone home to Zomba, Go and call Mandota the sergeant, To come and interpret; tell him this call is urgent. *(Dumpling runs to police station)*
Dumpling	That which you commanded, Sir, I have done, Mandota is already here. *(Enters Mandota)*
Mandota	*(Talking to the people)* I will take you before the Magistrate, There, each of you, stand straight, Arms lowered down and look humble, Standing before a white man is not simple.

	When you speak, do so in a supplicating manner
	Otherwise at you he will thunder.
	You there, come first.
	What is you name?
Wilson Zimba	My name is Mr. Zimba
Mandota	You-you-; don't speak like that.
	If the boss hears you say so he'll call you a rat,
	Just say my name is Zimba.
	(Facing the magistrate)
	Sir, here is the first man with a plea.
Mitchell	What is your name, native?
Zimba	My name is *(coughs)* Wilson Zimba.
	I started work at Bruce Estates cutting timber.
	Later Livingstone promoted me to an overseer.
	Now in this thirteenth year of my service
	He has dismissed me without notice.
	I have come to seek redress
	From Livingstone's injustice.
Mitchell	Why has he fired you?
Zimba	Trivial reasons, I did not do anything worth dismissal.
	No, none at all.
Mitchell	Say one by one of the reasons,
	It is I who will determine if indeed they were trivial.
Zimba	He has made a rule that no native
	Should wear a hat on the estate without his leave.
Mitchell	That command is simple to obey.
	What do you lose by keeping your hat that way?
Zimba	Not as simple as you assume, Resident Magistrate.
	To answer you in a manner direct and straight,
	The hat protects my skull from the blazing sun
	And it makes me feel I am a gentleman.
Mitchell	All white men insist that natives should not wear hats in their presence,
	Your complaint against Willie Livingstone is just nonsense.
	He dismissed you because you were disobedient.

	From the way I see you, you are also arrogant,
	This matter is closed, learn to obey your white master.
	Do you have anything else to say?

Zimba   He commands me to stop
Attending Chilembwe's devotional services of hope.

Mitchell   Did he tell you why?

Zimba   No, he didn't but I know why,
Chilembwe sent food to workers of Bruce Estates to eat.
On those Estates people toil from sunrise
Without food, without rest, their energy totally diminished,
It is as if for some reason they are being punished,
By sending food to those famished people
Chilembwe was teaching by a simple
Example, how an employer should treat his workers,
But Livingstone took this amiss,
So he forbade us having contacts
With Chilembwe under any circumstances.
When I objected he fired me.
This is plain injustice as you can see.

Mitchell   Every employer has rules;
Those employees who disregard such rules are fools.
Go away, you deserve the dismissal.

Zimba   Not at all.

Mandota   *(Pushing Zimba aside)* The magistrate has said, go,
At once do so.

Zimba   Don't touch my suit,
It cost me quite a lot.
(Another man comes along)

(Enter Chimbiya, M'maniwa, Nzima)

Chimbiya   We have the same complaint, we three,
We all look sickly as you can see,
All because of Jarvis Livingstone.
With his whip he has broken my hip bone.
Most of the day I have to lie
On my stomach, no need to ask why.

	My haunches are dreadfully painful, No matter how I try to be careful When sitting Or sleeping.
Mitchell	All you three say that Mr. Livingstone has beaten you And that you have done nothing wrong. I don't believe what you say, Just go away.

(Re-enters Zimba)

Zimba	Sir, I have come back Not to talk about my unfair sack, But at their request, to help these two, The little girl and her mother too.
Mitchell	What lies are you going to tell me on their behalf.
Zimba	Not lies, Sir, But perfect truth.
Mitchell	Alright, go ahead.
Zimba	At the turn of the last century I was in the army With Mr. Mwamadi, father of this girl. In diligence and loyalty Mwamadi used to excel, As members of the Kings African Rifles we went to the Gold Coast Where we fought against the brave Ashanti and tried to get them accept British rule. It was there that Mwamadi was killed. My friend died a brave soldier's death Leaving behind his widow and child And his own widowed mother in poor health In a hamlet and on a piece of land Which Bruce now claims to be his. Mwamadi's widow unfortunately also died A year ago leaving the old woman and the little girl alone. The little girl got a job as a nursemaid Caring for the daughter of Mr. and Mrs. Livingstone. They have just dismissed her From the job she needed so badly,

	At the very time they have evicted her grandmother.
	The two have nothing to eat and nowhere to go
	Having been jettisoned like excess cargo
	For a trivial offence and failure to provide labour rent
	For help they appeal to you, Mr. Resident.
Mitchell	Why was the girl dismissed?
	And why was her grand mother evicted?
Zimba	She says-
Mitchell	Was the girl able to speak
	To her master direct?
Zimba	Yes, Sir.
Mitchell	Let her open her mouth,
	Maybe out of it may come some truth.
	Speak, girl, don't be afraid.
Zione	Nyasa, my master's daughter,
	Went running after her father in the field
	Without a helmet on her head.
	The *bwana* became angry with me.
Mitchell	What do you want me to do?
Zione	What you can do I don't know,
	What I know is that I am helpless.
Mitchell	What your *bwana* said was true.
	It is dangerous for white children to go bareheaded
	Under the hot tropical sun and when the sky is blue.
	You were guilty of neglecting your duty,
	That is why he dismissed you.
	In matters of dismissal there is nothing I can do.
	Go and look for another *bwana*
	To employ you as nursemaid of his *mwana*.
	Next!
Old woman	*(Mumbling)* Bwana Lishiton- haj-chased
	(Because she cannot understand, Zimba intervenes)
Zimba	She does the hard work herself, poor old woman,
	Because those she depended upon have gone ahead,

	By which I mean they are dead.
Mitchell	She must comply with the wishes of her landlord.
Zimba	But she is too old.
Mitchell	Enough, go away. I am not going to waster time on matters like these on a busy day.
	(Outside)
Zilongolola	Suppose we go to our chiefs And lay before them our cases and griefs.
Zimba	What is a chief these days but a glorified government messenger, I have a suggestion that is better. Let us go to our God-chosen leader, John Chilembwe. He is just across the River Mbombwe.
All	Let us go, let's go To Chilembwe, ho-ho-ho!

Scene II

Mitchell, Dumpling, Policeman, Jamali, Khumbanyiwa, O'Brien, Firewood women

Dumpling	All of you sit down there where it is cool. Not here, you fool? When the Magistrate enters, all of you must stand up, If you don't, I will give you a slap. *(Mitchell enters, Dumpling shouts)* All stand up. *(They stand up, some trembling)*
Policeman	The first accused is the man called Jamali. He comes from a village called Selemani in Njuli.
Mitchell	Read the charge.
Policeman	The ranger found Jamali in the Game Reserve with a gun shooting wild game, The gun is there as an exhibit,

	So are the animals he killed, a deer and a rabbit. Jamali has committed the offence Of poaching. This is against the Game Reserve Ordinance.
Mitchell	Accused, do you plead guilty?
Jamali	I don't plead guilty.
Mitchell	Do you deny that you killed The animals exhibited there?
Jamali	I don't deny, but What I refuse to admit is that To kill a wild animal Is an offence, no, not at all. The forest belongs to God Who has allowed man to hunt there since days of old.
Mitchell:	Government has made a law forbidding hunting in the Game Reserve. Those who break the law get the punishment they deserve.
Jamali:	I did not know There was such a law.
Mitchell:	Ignorance is no defence, According to the law you are just guilty of the offence. For this you must pay a one-pound fine. Until you pay the fine I impound the gun.
Jamali:	The gun is not mine.
Mitchell:	Who is the owner?
Jamali:	Reverend John Chilembwe Of the Providence Industrial Mission across the River Mbombwe. He sent me to hunt wild game for the meat Which school boarders like to eat.
Mitchell:	By lending the gun to you Chilembwe has committed an offence too. He will not have the gun Back till he has paid his own fine.
Jamali:	Will you let me go and see

| | If the Reverend can help me
Pay my fine and explain about the gun.
I'll soon be back, I'll not walk but run. |
|---|---|
| **Mitchell**: | Nonsense, you are now a prisoner.
Until you pay the fine I can't let you go anywhere.
(Turning towards the messengers)
Take this man to prison, Dumpling
Where he should start serving
His sentence until he has paid the fine.
If he does not pay by nine o'clock tomorrow,
Have his head trimmed
As is required of all those who are imprisoned. |
| **Mitchell:** | *(Facing women firewood collectors)*
Do you plead guilty? |
| **Spokeswoman:** | Why should we say no?
Forgive us *Bwana,* we didn't know the law. |
| **Mitchell:** | Ignorance is no defence,
Collecting firewood in that forest is an offence.
For five days you will cut grasses
Here at the *boma* using cutlasses.
Next time you are caught again
I will have to detain
You in prison where you will serve
The kind of sentence you deserve. |
| **Spokeswoman:** | May we take the firewood with us home, Sir. |
| **Mitchell:** | No. It will be used here.
(The court is closed) |

Scene III

Characters: *Khumbanyiwa, village headman*
Masiye, wife of Khumbanyiwa,
Somba, Clerk interpreter,
Mitchell, Resident Magistrate
Dumpling, Messenger
O'Brien, a white farm manager

Somba: *(Knocks at the Resident's door.)*

Resident: Come in.
What do you want, James?

Somba: The man who wants to see you,
Sir, says his problem is too
Big for anyone but you.

Resident: Bring him in.

Khumbanyiwa: Certain things white people have done to me I don't understand,
Whether there in Mozambique or here in Nyasaland.
I am village headman Khumbanyiwa
With a village and piece of land at Namiwawa,
Near the farm owned by a white man called Brown.
He has employed there a drunken manager called O'Brien.
This man is a threat to my life
Just because of my younger wife.

Mitchell: Alright, sit down outside and wait there,
I will send for the Manager.
Dumpling take this letter to O'Brien
Run, it's an urgent matter.

O'Brien: *(O'Brien arrives)*
Have you summoned me, Mitchell?
Why?

Mitchell: I sent for you, Mr. O'Brien
Because this village headman

	Says you are threatening his life
	On account of his younger wife.
	(Turning to Khumbanyiwa)
	Now continue with your story.
Khumbanyiwa:	O'Brien has often insulted me after he has drunk too much beer
	Yesterday he went too far by demanding that I surrender my dear
	Younger wife to him to be his mistress.
	His very words caused me a lot of distress.
	When I refused he warned me I would lose my life
	All this on account of my younger wife.
	May I know from you Mr. Resident Magistrate
	If such behaviour is crooked or straight?
Mitchell:	It is crooked not straight.
	(Turning to O'Brien)
	Well, O'Brien you have heard
	What the village headman has said.
O'Brien:	Well, so what?
	Can't you see how lovely she is to look at?
	I don't mind her colour or her nose,
	My eyes follow her wherever she goes.
Mitchell:	What you say is scandalous,
	And could lead to something disastrous.
	You lower the respect for the European that the native
	Has by saying things that are naive,
	Your behaviour is a source of shame
	And you are not worth an Irish name.
O'Brien:	Don't be sanctimonious, Philip Mitchell,
	You have sins enough to take you to hell.
	Don't people snatch other men's wives in Britain?
	Nay, in France, Germany, Holland, or Spain?
	What do you expect us white men
	To do here where there are too few white women?
	To seize the women of a conquered race
	Is an old tradition, a virtue, not a disgrace.
	The natives themselves have been doing to each other

	The very things about which you bother.
Mitchell:	Be satisfied with the one Black woman you already have, Leave the headman's wife alone.
O'Brien:	I am a British subject I have the freedom to associate With anybody even another man's wife I don't mind what happens to my life.
Mitchell:	This last I have to say: Right from today Keep away from the headman's wife, And don't threaten his life. Otherwise I'll draw the matter to the Governor's attention Who might order your deportation.

Scene IV

Characters: Khumbanyiwa, Maggie, Khumbanyiwa's wife, Somba, Dumpling, Mitchell, O'Brien, Zimba, Villagers

Villagers:	*(In a procession to the Resident)* Ho-ho-ho, we have seized the dangerous man O'Brien, He has killed Khumbanyiwa's child with his deadly gun. Ho-ho-ho, let us take him to the Resident And demand that he be given severe punishment.
O'Brien:	Leave me alone, you bloody savages.
Villages:	Tie the white beast farmer, ho-ho-ho! Don't mind what he says, to the Resident we go. And take with us the body of the child That with his muzzle gun he has killed.
Maggie:	*(Weeping as they approach Resident)* My daughter, Koneni, what have you done That the white man should kill you with a gun? Lord Jesus say to my daughter *talitha cumi*, Without Koneni life will be nothing to me.

(They arrive at the Resident's office)

Mitchell: What is all this?
A white man tied with ropes!
How dare you do such a thing you bloody people?
No matter what he has done, treat any white man as a noble.

Zimba: What you see lying on the mat there
Wrapped in a sack cloth
Is the dead body of Khumbanyiwa's daughter.
O'Brien must account for her murder.

Mitchell: Untie the white master first,
What you have done to him is unjust.
For he is presumed free and innocent
Until he is pronounced guilty by a Resident.

Zimba: We decided to tie him with ropes
Because his behaviour was dashing our hopes
Of persuading him to come here at all
And stand before you the Magistrate for trial.

Mitchell: Untie him and quickly too.
(They untie O'Brien)
O'Brien, come and take a seat
On this chair away from dust and heat.

O'Brien: Thank you. *(Takes a seat)*

Mitchell: How are you found in this strange situation,
Natives howling around you with commotion?
Your arms tied behind your back,
What do you say about the dead body of a child lying there in the sack?

O'Brien: For this incident my gun is responsible.
All this was by accident pure and simple.

Mitchell: How did the accident happen?

O'Brien: I take shooting lessons in the Phalombe Plain
Together with twenty other white men.
Preparing ourselves to meet the Kaiser's men.
There in the shooting exercise Collin Grant

	Does it the manner I can't. He has been laughing at me For the clumsy manner I handle the gun, you see. I swore one day I would demonstrate My marksmanship by shooting an actual beast. Then they all would say "O'Brien, You too are a worthy man."
Mitchell:	Come to the point, O'Brien I can't afford to remain here until the setting sun, I have to go to Blantyre to play golf With Willie Livingstone, say the rest in brief.
O'Brien:	What you say is impertinent. Am I to expect justice from you, Resident?
Mitchell	Give me the facts. In my turn I will give you the justice.
O'Brien	Then don't interrupt me.
Mitchell	Go ahead.
O'Brien	On Brown's farm there's a fig tree, Birds and squirrels go up there on the succulent fruits nibbling with glee. Today after a brief stare I saw something like a monkey up the tree there, I said this is my chance to use the gun to good effect. I touched the trigger letting a bullet Out. In a moment something came down yelling And shortly the natives came shouting. Before I could explain I found With ropes they had got me bound.
Mitchell	But how could you not see That it was a human child up the tree?
O'Brien	Oh, come on, be realistic, Mitchell, Do I have to tell You that black children When they are seen At a distance resemble monkeys? How often have we whites called natives apes.

Mitchell	*(Addressing the complainants)* Village headman Khumbanyiwa, I am sorry for what happened there at Namiwawa. Mr. O'Brien did not kill your child Intentionally, but mistook it for something wild. I cannot therefore charge him with murder, But a less serious homicide called manslaughter.
Khumbanyiwa	Sir, please do not believe what O'Brien has said for I know that Since the day I brought him here For trying to do something evil with my dear Mayeso, he has been threatening my life. No doubt he has killed my child because of my younger wife.
Mitchell	O'Brien is tried according to English law, Not native customary law, Which is so crude that every homicide it treats as murder. What O'Brien has done is not murder but manslaughter, For this offence he deserves only a fine And to pay the bereaved some compensation. *(Turning towards O'Brien)* As for you, the accused, be more careful with your gun, Otherwise natives will regard you as a cruel man. They might do to you something worse than they have done today. Before I pronounce the sentence do you have anything to say?
O'Brien	No.
Mitchell	For what you have done, You must pay one pound as a fine. Another pound as compensation to the father and mother Of the child; this will be the end of the matter.
O'Brien	Oh God, two pounds, that's terrible Unfair punishment for accidentally shooting dead a child of a black couple.
Mitchell	If you like, appeal to the high court And risk a stiffer verdict.

O'Brien	I am not going to appeal To men from whom I can't expect a square deal. But can you lend me three quids, Two to pay for the offence I have been fined, The third to buy a bottle of sherry. I will pay back the lot when Brown has paid me my salary.
Mitchell	No, the best I can do Is to allow you To bring the fine on the day You are going to get your pay.
O'Brien	Oh, Mitchell You are hell. *(Departs)*
Mitchell	Khumbanyiwa, go home straight And there wait For message from this office To come and collect the compensation for the loss.
Zimba	For a loss like this do you consider one pound a fair assessment? It's a mere mockery, not compensation, Mr. Resident.
Mitchell	But why are you questioning my judgement? O'Brien did not kill your child.
Zimba	Khumbanyiwa is a friend of mine We eat *nsima* and drink together our native wine. I am bound to do what Chilembwe has said, That all the time Africans should stand side by side, Give each other a helping hand; This is why here I stand.
Mitchell	Just clear off, cheeky mission native! What Chilembwe has told you is naive, If you open your mouth once again, On you I'll impose a heavier fine.
Zimba	My friend Khumbanyiwa, let us go to John Chilembwe Beyond the River Mbombwe And lay before him our sorrows, Then see what follows.

Scene V

Mitchell, Somba, Dumpling

Mitchell Fetch the register of village headmen.
We should see if Khumbanyiwa and his men
Have paid this year's taxes
Which they must do at all costs.

Somba *(Having looked into the register, brings it)*
The register shows Khumbanyiwa paid his tax in nineteen
Twelve and this year is nineteen fourteen.

Mitchell Gosh, why did my predecessor not collect the taxes?
The government needs the money it can get for administrative costs.
Every native that has a wife and a hut
Must pay a tax, some of the money is required this year to pay soldiers departing for combat.
I understand the Huns just now are across the River Songwe,
If they cross it they will soon be at the River Lilongwe.
All the way ruthlessly slaughtering you natives
As they did in the Maji Maji war with their rebellious natives

Somba To hell with Germans and their Kaiser!
For us natives the British and King George are better.

Mitchell You are a loyal native worth rewarding.
By the way, where is Dumpling?
The campaign for tax collection must start today for the people of Namiwawa,
And confront litigious Khumbanyiwa.

Somba I saw Dumpling a while ago with a mat
Oh his shoulder heading for this hut.

Mitchell Go and fetch him!

(Dumpling arrives panting)

Mitchell Dumpling, you and Mandota, this afternoon,
Take with you a receipt book and a gun
To village headman Khumbanyiwa,

| | Not the one at Nsoni but at Namiwawa.
Command him and his men to pay the taxes,
The government needs the money at once. |
|---|---|
| *Dumpling* | As you command, Sir, there will I go today,
It is my duty without question to obey. |
| *Mitchell* | Arrest those who refuse or fail to pay,
Bring them here in chains,
Those who are uppity,
And those who are haughty,
Burn their houses,
Uproot their crops.
All is fair in times like these ones
When our lives are threatened by the Kaiser's Huns |

Scene VI

Mitchell, Zimba, Somba, Khumbanyiwa, Maggie, Mayeso, Villagers

| *Mitchell* | Go to the post office, Somba,
And find out if there is mail from Zomba.
Oh, what noise is about outside!
It is so loud that Mrs. Bryce and I here inside
Cannot hear each other.
Go and tell the natives to shut up there. |
|---|---|
| *Somba* | Yes, Sir.
(Somba goes out of the office) |
| *Villagers* | Ho-ho-ho we have caught
The ravisher in the abominable act;
Ho-ho-ho the *boma* messenger
Is not a genuine tax collector but a wife-snatcher. |
| *Somba* | Listen you people, listen please;
The Resident commands you to stop the noise.
If you don't shut up he will put you all in jail
Where you'll have a taste of hell.
(Sees Dumpling) Now, now what do I see
That almost blinds me? |

Zimba	What's wrong with your eyes, brother? That which you see here is nothing else but Dumpling, the messenger Whom the Resident sent to Namiwawa To collect taxes, but has injured headman Khumbanyiwa
Somba	What offence has Dumpling committed That you bring him back naked with ropes tied?
Zimba	When we caught him in the dirty act he was like this. He was not wearing his shorts. We will use his trousers as an exhibit To prove that what we accuse him of he really did it.
Somba	Then wait a bit, my boss Is having a chat with Mrs. Bryce.
Zimba	What sort of a man is the Resident, Chatting in a room alone with somebody's wife While the husband is not around but absent? Is this not how to start a strife?
Villager 1	Indeed two of them Within a locked room. Ha-ha-ha, heh, heh, heh.
Villager 2	What sort of justice can we expect From a Magistrate who does not respect Another man's exclusive rights to his wife? Well, well, to be married is to have difficult life.
Zimba	Never mind, justice today against the knave At all costs we must have.
Somba	Ah, now they seem to be free. That lady you see Coming out there is Mrs. Bryce As usual looking slim and spruce.
Zimba	Go and tell the Magistrate then That we are here to see him again.
Somba	A riddle has taken place, Sir, Dumpling, your favourite messenger Boasted he would return from the tax campaigns

	With tax defaulters in chains,
	But the villagers have brought him back a captive
	And in a condition most humiliating you have to see to believe.
Mitchell	Go, and bring them here.
Somba	Here is Khumbanyiwa
	Whom you already know as headman at Namiwawa.
Mitchell	Ah, it is you Khumbanyiwa, a typical native
	Fond of *milandu*, litigation and anything naïve.
	Why have you brought here my messenger in a manner so unseemly?
	Untie him. Give him back his clothes. Do so quickly.
Zimba	Do not be overheated, Mr. Resident.
	Of a crime big or small we are innocent
	Instead of threatening us,
	Hear us without anger or prejudice.
Mitchell	Speak then you cheeky mission school native.
Zimba	Khumbanyiwa, the main victim, will speak first.
	His first wife Maggie will speak next.
	His second wife Mayeso will speak third.
	I'll then just add a word.
	Up to you Khumbanyiwa,
	Village headman of Namiwawa.
Khumbanyiwa	Two men, including the one we have brought here half naked,
	Came to my village looking arrogant and proud.
	They demanded that I and my people pay taxes.
	At the same time ordered all of us
	To bring *nsima* and chicken in a pot,
	Some beer and what would constitute a banquet.
	Having enjoyed our hospitality,
	That man Dumpling became more uppity,
	He said you Khumbanyiwa and your people are mere rats,
	Why have you not yet paid the taxes
	For the year nineteen thirteen
	And also the year nineteen fourteen?

Bring the tax money, now, now or else
I'll burn each defaulter's house,
We pleaded, thus. "Give us time today to go and borrow
The money from relatives; we will pay the taxes tomorrow."
He ordered us to surrender to him our wives,
So that he could keep them as hostages.
I have two wives.
Glancing at my younger wife with covetous eyes
He said to me "You with grey hair,
You do not deserve a woman so young, so fair."
I replied "Say what you like, she is still mine
Daily she prepares the meal that I dine."
He eyed me sourly
Before saying "God and find the tax money quickly."
He was holding a gun and a big knife.
I got frightened for my life.
So I hastily departed. What happened after I had gone,
I will leave my senior wife briefly to explain.

Maggie We women were thirty in number.
Twenty of us were herded together
In my house
Others were taken to Kalima's.
The one guarding our group was that man called Dumpling.
He had a gun, a knife and something
Else I can't remember. My house was not big enough
To accommodate twenty persons; we found it too rough,
Lying side by side there inside.
We longed for permission to go outside.
"Now that I have eaten your food
I must taste your bodies to see if they are just as good."
Said Dumpling, such things and we wondered if he was a cannibal.
But soon it was clear to us all
As he peeped into my face and said 'old and ugly'.
He then peeped into Mayeso's face and said this one is comely;
Let us have fun.

	Here let me end my part,
	Mayeso, my co-wife, may start.
Mayeso	When that man over there ordered me to undress
	I felt a good deal of distress.
	I gasped, shook my head and said what!
	I do not lie down flat
	For any other man but my husband.
	The language of adultery I don't understand,
	Go and sleep with your own wife.
	He said, "Don't be rude, otherwise you will lose your life."
	When my fellow inmates heard
	This they said 'you better yield'.
	We know you do not want to cuckold
	Your husband, but as a captive you cannot afford
	To be morally prim; submit, it's not your fault at all."
	Dumpling then nudged me into a gentle fall.
	Having spoken this far
	I leave it to Zimba to continue from there.
Zimba	I arrived at Namiwawa with my colleague Jamali.
	We had been instructed by the great John Chilembwe that after visiting Njuli
	We should call upon Khumbanyiwa
	With a special message for him and his people at Namiwawa.
	When we arrived it was dark,
	But quiet, we did not even hear a dog bark.
	As we approached Khumbanyiwa's main
	House, we saw a woman bearing a gun
	A bit clumsily and also a pair of trousers.
	We recognized her with the help of lights.
	She was Maggie, Khumbanyiwa's senior wife.
	I asked her what she was doing outside.
	She said 'go and see what's happening inside'.
	We pushed the door aside.
	Ho, there was Dumpling lying naked
	On top of Mayeso who looked as if she was dead.
	We pounced on the thief,
	As we usually call someone who despoils somebody's wife.

Mitchell	*(Facing Dumpling)* What do you say to the accusation That you forced each villager to give you a chicken?
Dumpling	These people are talking like children. I asked them for only one chicken.
Mitchell	What about the other accusation, Raping Khumbanyiwa's wife, Having threatened her life?
Dumpling	I do not deny That these men found me with trousers down, That I did lie Down on the mat With that lovely woman over there. I did not use force. When I told her I was going to give her money She heaved a sigh of joy and called me honey. Raping Khumbanyiwa's wife Having threatened her life?
Mitchell	Well, Mayeso, you have heard What Dumpling has said.
Mayeso	What has come out of his mouth Is the opposite of truth.
Mitchell	*(Facing the messenger)* What you have done, Dumpling, is in Breach of discipline. You are not supposed to demand hospitality, Neither to deprive any female hostage of her chastity, You are authorized only to detain tax defaulters' wives, But not to threaten their lives. Before I pronounce a sentence on You, do you have anything to say in mitigation?
Dumpling	My wife has a small baby, Our custom says that a daddy Should not have sex with the mother In case he injures the child's tender Health. Hence for several months since the child's birth I have lived a life without mirth, And when I saw that young beauty

	With her stork neck which makes her look extra pretty,
	I couldn't resist the temptation.
	This is my plea for mitigation.
Mitchell	Despite what you have said
	I am not much amused.
	For the offence of lying on the mat
	With Khumbanyiwa's wife without
	Her consent I sentence you to six months imprisonment.
	This sentence is quite lenient.
	For three of these months you will be an outdoor prisoner.
	The other three you will be serving while you are a soldier.
	You will be sent to Karonga on half pay,
	Where I shall be with you one day.
	Both of us will be attached to the Kings African Rifles 1st Battalion
	Where you will continue to be under my supervision.
Khumbanyiwa	Is this justice?
Mitchell	Perfect justice.
Zimba	How can you say that, Sir?
	Promoting a ravisher into a soldier,
	This is ridiculous.
Mitchell	If you say that again,
	I'll detain
	You in jail for contempt
	Of His Majesty's court
Zimba	But
Khumbanyiwa	I have seen people going across the River Mbombwe
	With their problems to see John Chilembwe.
	But to me it seems just a waste of time
	What I have failed to get here, how can I get it from him?
Zimba	Chilembwe is a leader every black person should trust
	For those who want help, going to him is a must.
	He has been to America and England
	Come with, me dear friends, to the leader of Nyasaland.
	He knows the white man's ways in and out,
	He will give us the attention we need; have no doubt.

Scene VII

Characters: *Chilembwe, Mrs. Ida Chilembwe, persons with problems*
Mlauli, Village headman
Numero, Demobilized soldier
Khumbanyiwa, Village headman
Others, Stephen, Mkulichi, David Kaduya

Mrs. Chilembwe	Father of John Junior
Chilembwe	Yes, mother of John Junior
Mrs. Chilembwe	More men and women have arrived. Most of them looking haggard and starved, Each with his or her problem. Why, darling do you encourage them To believe that in you they will find solutions To their heart-rending tribulations?
Chilembwe	They come to you and me Because with their own eyes they see How here at the PIM we do care For our people's welfare.
Mrs. Chilembwe	To feel sympathy with someone's problems is nice, To be able to solve those problems is something else, The burdens of the PIM are for you heavy enough. Darling, you have neither adequate materials nor staff To accomplish The work you so much relish. So why take on extra burdens? You will just bring upon yourself unnecessary strains; Your health of late has not been at its best I dare say you need a bit of rest.
Chilembwe	When I am working alone I feel pain in the head and the backbone. But when you are nearby I don't feel any kind of stress Even when I am clearing a lot of mess.
Mrs. Chilembwe	In that case I must come and join you, Maybe there will be something for me to do.

Chilembwe	You will be most welcome indeed,
	For you will enforce my other group of advisors David Kaduya,
	Stephen Mkulichi, Wilson Zimba and other friends-in-need,
	You might understand each woman's problem
	Better since you are lucky enough to be one of them.
Mrs. Chilembwe	Do you think it is lucky to be a woman?
Chilembwe	Indeed it is, especially if that woman is you.
	Come with me then, darling, please do.
	(They go outside where people have gathered in front of Chilembwe's house)
Mlauli	My name is Mlauli,
	I am a village headman in Njuli.
	My people and I live on ancestral land,
	Fertile and free from any grain of sand.
	Several times Bruce has tried to encroach
	On my land; now he has sent his assistant called Roach,
	Accompanied by a black servant's band.
	They are surveying my land.
	I and my people do not want *thangata* serfdom.
	Poor as we are we want to retain our freedom
	To cultivate the land we own,
	To reap for ourselves the seeds we have sown.
	Reverend Chilembwe, you know better the ways of the white men.
	What should we do, I and my men?
Chilembwe	Villagers on the Highlands who under *thangata* groan
	Blame their chiefs and headmen
	For saying yes, Sir, to everything a whiteman said.
	Gone now is the time for blind obeisance,
	You and your people must resort to defiance
	When Bruce's man Roach and his unruly band
	Return to trespass on your land.
Mlauli	With what can we defy, Sir?
Chilembwe	With the means most appropriate to the occasion.
	(Turning to his advisors)
	Well, lady and gentlemen, if my advice is wrong, say so

	I don't pretend everything to know.
Stephen Mkulichi	Your advice is right.
Kaduya	With spears and axes Mlauli and his men should go and fight. These are the appropriate means of defiance. It does not help to suffer in silence.
Chilembwe	There is no need to fight and kill Someone if there is still The opportunity that by negotiation We can find a solution. What is your view, Ida, my dear? Time is ripe for women to speak without fear.
Mrs. Chilembwe	I agree with you, it is wrong to fight When we can get things right By talking and discussing over matters. War turns wives and children to widows and orphans.
Mkulichi	We must excuse our brother Kaduya, As a British soldier he fought in Somalia. Truly has it been said, Once a soldier you remain a soldier till you are dead.
Kaduya	You may be right there Mkulichi, I'm afraid, My heart still longs for the battle field, Whoever grabs our ancestral land Deserves to be killed like an eland. *(Turning to Mlauli)* However for the time being Mlauli heed what the Reverend has said; we'll wait and see the end. *(Exit Mlauli)*
Chilembwe	Next.
Jamali	This is Corporal Numero from the Bruce estates at Magomero.
Chilembwe	Don't force yourself to stand up, Corporal Numero.
Numero	As a soldier I ought To present myself before you, Sir, standing upright, But you are right, the best I can do is squat down.

I've but one leg, a sad thing for a valiant man,
I am unable to salute with my right hand
On which there remain only two fingers and
A thumb. Behind every queer thing there is a story.
As I tell mine, all of you will feel sorry.
For me in the year eighteen ninety nine
I was sent to Somalia and fought on the front line,
With dedication I served Queen Victoria,
As I fought I joined in singing Rule Britannia.
From Somalia we went to the Gold Coast.
None of the battles we had so far fought
Were as fierce as those against the Ashanti.
They are terrible fighters, those people, so are their fellow
    Akan, the Fanti.
Many of my colleagues were wounded, but I managed to
    come back without a scratch.
Then three months ago in the month of March
I was sent North to join those who wanted to capture New
    Langenburg
From Kaiser's soldiers and drink German beer there just
    brought in from Hamburg.
Our army commander had assured us all
That kicking out the Germans would be as easy as kicking
    off a football.
But that turned out to be a great lie.
It was not the Germans and their blacks who that day did
    die
In large numbers but us. Lettow von Vorbeck,
The German Commander, has the swiftness of a spring
    bolt,
The ferocity and strength of a lion.
In no time he pushed back the First Battalion
Of the King's African Rifles.
Once more I was a bit luckier than others
In that I lost only my leg and the two fingers.
Since I could no longer fight I was discharged,
Not very honourably, since I was sent back empty handed
To my hamlet on Bruce's Magomero estate,
Only to find my family in a wretched estate,

	Evicted for failure to do full *thangata* work.
	With difficulty I journeyed by hoping
	To see the Resident; breathless but hoping,
	He would persuade Livingstone and Bruce
	To let me remain on the land as a reward for my military service,
	Mitchell just said come next Tuesday,
	Today I am too busy anyway.
	I have been to see him again and again,
	All my efforts have ended in vain,
	But the Resident has resettled his fellow white man Eric Brown
	Who was wounded with me
	On a thousand acres of land, he is growing tea and coffee.
Chilembwe	Yours is a sad story indeed.
	What your employers promised by word they should now fulfill in deed.
	(Turning to colleagues)
	Do you have something to say, Kaduya?
	You once fought for Queen Victoria.
Kaduya	What you have heard is not an isolated case,
	Many ex-soldiers are treated like this.
	When they are healthy and fit
	They are given food and urged to fight,
	But when they are wounded
	They are sent back on poor rations and then abandoned.
	Thank God, I got my discharge before suffering loss
	Of my limbs and arms.
	I have these organs with me still intact.
	One day I will use them to fight
	Those who mistreat us.
	On that day they will realize I am a bull not an ass.
Chilembwe	Numero, as a man who fought for the British empire,
	The British should give you special care.
	Vigorously I will go and plead for you with the Resident,
	Failing which I will proceed to Zomba, the seat of Government.
	To see the Government with my petition

	That you should be given freehold land of your own.
Chilembwe	Next.
Zimba	Sir, this is Khumbanyiwa, Headman at Namiwawa.
Chilembwe	Oh, I see, welcome Headman. I have long wanted to see you gentleman. Let us hear what you have to say On this rather gloomy day.
Khumbanyiwa	I left my home near Namuli Hill Because of troubles which threatened to kill Me. This was in the year eighteen eighty. The year Portuguese oppression of the Lomwe was at its height. First white people to come to Lomwe country were Scotch. They came to Murumbu to teach and preach They taught us to sing what a friend We have in Jesus and God save Queen Victoria. We saw them clap hands and say Rule Britannia. Most of the time it was John Grey Kufa who taught Us to sing, read and write. How we loved him is more than I can tell.
Chilembwe	Have you found in Nyasaland the freedom That you lost in your old home?
Khumbanyiwa	If telling a lie is a sin Then let me tell the truth about myself and kin. You have heard of how a white man accosted me about my young wife; When I answered in anger he threatened my life. Later he shot dead my daughter who was in a tree Fetching fruits that God had given mankind free. To cut the story short What I came to fetch in Nyasaland I have not yet got. I am still wandering in the wilderness Of afflictions, but no redress. I don't know how you can help me, I am a wretched man as you can see.

Chilembwe	Evidently you have been through hell. 'T's time I go and see Resident Phillip Mitchell That without delay justice be done To each and everyone. *(Turning aside)* Jamali is there another one?
Jamali	Reverend here is an elderly woman Whose face suggests she is care worn. Her name is Nazimbiri, She comes from the village of Sikumbiri.
Nazimbiri	The young man has correctly introduced me, That I am a woman of sorrows it is easy to see, Recently my life has been put into hell By the resident at Chiradzulu *boma* called Mitchell. He has taken away my only son to join the war and die, Leaving me with nobody on whom to rely.
Chilembwe	Yours is indeed a sad story, oh, woman of Africa. You are like other women whose sons and daughters were taken to America, Never to be seen by their mothers again. Admittedly forced separation of a woman from her son causes life long pain *(Turns to Ida Chilembwe)* Do you want to say something, mother of John Junior?
Mrs. Chilembwe	Yes, father of John Junior.
Chilembwe	By all means go ahead. Where women's problems are concerned Lady leaders understand them better.
Mrs. Chilembwe	Mai Nazimbiri, we have missed you in the catechumen class For quite a few Sundays. I did not know you had all these problems.
Nazimbiri	From the time the recruiter took my son away, My landlord's foreman came to me to say: Go and finish the *thangata* work that your son began. I said, oh foreman, can't you see I am an old woman? Where can I get the strength to do such work

	He glared at me before he began to bark;
	"If you disobey my command
	My *bwana* will evict you from his land."
	For fear of being driven away
	I go and toil *thangata*.
	Whenever I fail to finish a day's assignment,
	The foreman writes on my ticket 'absent.'
	No credit is given
	For what I have done.
	By the end of the week I feel bodily stresses
	And lack strength to come here for Sunday services.
Mrs. Chilembwe	*(Turning to her husband)*
	Darling, you have heard
	The rest of what she has said.
Chilembwe	Thank you, Ida, for enlisting more information
	From Nazimbiri which has deepened my compassion.
	(Turning to Nazimbiri)
	Tomorrow I will go and see the Resident Mitchell
	To release you son. What he will say I cannot tell
	In advance, but I will do my best.
	Meanwhile go home and have a bit of rest.

Scene VIII

At Chiradzulu Boma

Chilembwe   *(Looking at his watch)*
                    We have arrived ten minutes before the appointed time.
                    It is quite a distance whence we have come.

Zimba   But I will be surprised, pastor,
                    If the Resident invites us in on time. So far,
                    As I have had the experience with Mitchell,
                    When it comes to appointments he makes Blacks wait like
                       hell.

Chilembwe   Let us wait and see.
                    My duty is to solve any problem, whatever that may be.

Zimba	There comes Somba. Mitchell's right hand man from Zomba.
Somba	Good morning Reverend Chilembwe, How is everything beyond the River Mbombwe?
Chilembwe	Good morning fellow country man. Nothing is okay in this land for any black man or woman. That's why we have come here to see Resident Mitchell To talk about matters that are not being handled well. Go then and inform him. We have arrived on time.
Somba	That will I do, It's a pleasure to serve you. *(He knocks at the Resident's Office)* Reverend Chilembwe has arrived.
Mitchell	Reverend who?
Somba	John Chilembwe of the PIM. He says you have an appointment with him.
Mitchell	*(Scanning his diary)* Oh yes, the pastor of a native church That mixes magic with Christianity so much. Tell him to wait, I have to attend to the white man first.
Somba	They started talking about cricket, Then they talked of matters more secret. Later they enthused about golf, They chatted about horses and the turf. They made references to the war against the Kaiser, And about how many natives they have recruited so far.
Chilembwe	To me all those matters are trivial, That which concerns my people is special, Grievances unattended to for too long Make everything else go wrong. Once more about us go and remind him. Everything is done best when it is done on time.
Somba	Be patient, Sir, Bwana Mitchell has a bad temper.

Chilembwe	I can be patient with anything, But not with my people's suffering.
Mitchell	*(Standing at the door)* Somba, tell the native pastor to come in. *(Chilembwe and the colleague go in)* Are you the John Chilembwe I have been hearing about?
Chilembwe	I am the one, have no doubt.
Mitchell	In stature so small, Why are you not tall?
Chilembwe	Never mind my stature; it does me no harm; The Lord above decided that I should be just as I am. After all, was not Harry Johnston the first British ruler Of Nyasaland a man of small stature? Nevertheless he laid a foundation for you, The work that you and others do. I too will lay a foundation On which my unhappy people will build a happy nation. *(In walks Mrs. Bryce)*
Mitchell	Ah come in Dorothy, Good morning.
Mrs. Bryce	Good morning Phillip, I bring you Scones and chocolates too.
Mitchell	*(Facing Chilembwe)* Natives go out and wait, I must attend to a white lady first. *(Chilembwe scowls but walks out)*
Chilembwe	This is unjust, Having waited thirty minutes, part of me says go home and think Of other means to bring African freedom to the brink, But the other side says, have a bit of patience, Though never accept the suffering of your people in silence.
Zimba	Eh, Somba, our fellow Black, Why is your white boss holding us back? What is Mitchell talking with the woman whose husband has gone fighting

	In German East Africa, does he want to make her his darling?
Somba	That question I can't answer, I am afraid. Anyway, Mrs. Bryce has come out, Looking tall, almost upright.
Mrs. Bryce	*(Looking at Chilembwe and others)* Eh, Natives, cheer up, Why look so depressed?
Chilembwe and the rest	Because we are oppressed,
Mrs. Bryce	That's strange, let me go. *(Hurries off to the rickshaw)*
Mitchell	What have you come to say? Be quick I am extra busy today.
Chilembwe	I have two problems To which to draw your attention, Indeed for us both to find a solution. The first concerns the harassment of my people, The other is more personal though equally horrible.
Mitchell	Who are your people? Be specific and quickly, too! Are you an Nguru, Nyanja, Yao, what tribe are you?
Chilembwe	All those are my people, I make no tribal distinctions at all, I am just an African. My destiny is to achieve whatever I can, To give or seek help for all those in agony, Where there is conflict to bring about harmony.
Mitchell	Enough of that pretentious eloquence In which there is nothing that makes sense. Speak in brief, what do you want me to do About your people and yourself too?
Chilembwe	Living conditions of the African on private estates are very bad. None of my people is happy there, all very sad. At Magomero, on the estates of Bruce, Things are getting worse and worse.

Mitchell	No, they are not.
Chilembwe	They are. The general manager of the estate, Willie Livingstone, Has a heart harder than a stone. Widows whose husbands have died Fighting in German East Africa he has evicted From his land because they fail to do *thangata,* labour rent. Is this what you call justice, Mr. Resident?
Mitchell	I have heard that stuff before, All you are saying now is a bore. You natives are all liars by nature, No one is ill-treated anywhere in the British Empire.
Chilembwe	Apparently you have never been to Magomero, I suggest you go there tomorrow And see things for yourself That every African there has been turned into a serf.
Mitchell	For me to go there it would be a waste of time. What Willie Livingstone has told me is enough, I trust him. What you complain about is mere rubbish, Everything you natives do or say is childish.
Chilembwe	Won't you then do anything About my people's crying?
Mitchell	The trouble with you black people Is that you are never grateful For what we whites have done; we have brought you hospitals For instance, roads, bridges and schools. Be grateful to the white man for the burden He's shouldering to civilize you, Ham's grandchildren.
Chilembwe	The white man's burden is Carried on the black man's shoulders. No sooner than your predecessors claimed this country for Queen Victoria, Than took our soldiers to Mauritius and Somalia. From there they took them to the Ashanti

	Whose land your country wanted to annex like that of the Fanti. While our soldiers are far away, Fighting, killing and getting killed day by day, For causes they know not, For pay not even worth a milk pot, See how white people treat our soldiers' wives and children. You make them carry that which you call the white man's burden. Wives and widows of soldiers are compelled to pay taxes Doing *thangata,* using hoes and axes.
Mitchell	The Bruce Estate is private land On which Mr. Bruce enjoys the same rights as other landlords in Scotland. He has the right to evict those who trespass On his land for whatever purpose.
Chilembwe	What about the rights of a tenant?
Mitchell	A tenant must do all that he's told By his or her landlord. Otherwise he or she must quit and live elsewhere. Things must then rest there.
Chilembwe	But why did you destroy my school building That on communal land was standing?
Mitchell	You built it too close to the mission Of white people, this without their permission. They came and complained to me. You must respect white missionaries' rights, you see.
Chilembwe	But at least you should Have heard my side Of the story first. What you did was unjust.
Mitchell	What I have heard about your teaching Would justify burning The rest of your schools; They transform ignorant natives into dangerous fools.
Chilembwe	I teach my people nothing but the Bible truth

	And about the rights that God has given them since dates of their birth.
Mitchell	You teach them that Africa is for Africans, don't you?
Chilembwe	Well, that I do, Or else to whom does Africa belong?
Mitchell	Your teaching is wrong, Look at the map, beautifully painted as if with a brush; Red colour means all this British; Blue colour means all this French empire The Portuguese are in Mozambique, here and Angola there.
Chilembwe	If someone entered your house, Gun in hand, full of menace Claiming everything there as his by virtue of his might, Would you say that what he says is right?
Mitchell	We whites rule you blacks not only by the right of conquest, But also because in God's eyes we are the best Specimens of his image. Besides, from age to age Civilized people have ruled the uncivilized, The educated have ruled the uneducated. Be grateful, Chilembwe, we whites are not just here to rule but also to civilize you. God has given us this job to do.
Chilembwe	You are propounding racialist theories, That might make native people in British colonies Dissatisfied being subjects of the British Empire And try to bring nearer The day of their freedom Force the colonizers go back to their home.
Mitchell	Just stuff and nonsense, what you say. For two hundred years have we been in Bombay Calcutta, Madras, Bengal ruling the Indian. For half a millennium shall we be here to rule the African Native. Behold, when we went to India we found there traces of civilization.

	The Bunyans had invented a writing of their own.
But here in Africa we found no wheel or any type of craft,
Except such as has to do with witchcraft.
Mind you, the Bible says you as children of Ham
Are to be our servants; accept your role and be very calm.
Chilembwe	I reject everything you say.
The African wind is gathering strength day by day.
The African morning sun is on the horizon.
Sooner than later African freedom will be born.
Mitchell	Now I am convinced beyond doubt,
Chilembwe, you are a firebrand out and out,
Your schools are used for subversion.
It was a mistake you were given permission
To have schools of your own.
I will let the Governor know this. Now be gone.
Chilembwe	*(Standing up)* I came to ask for fair treatment of my people.
You have promised me nothing at all.
Mitchell	Get out of my office, obstinate native.

Act Three

Scene I

Joseph Booth, Chilembwe, Ida Chilembwe

Booth	John Chilembwe, John Chilembwe,
Come and meet me here by the River Mbombwe.
Chilembwe	Who is calling me?
Booth	Come nearer and see.
Chilembwe	Ah, it is you, my uncle Joseph Booth,
The man who taught me God's truth.
When did you come back

	To this land of humiliation for those who are coloured black?
Booth	I have slipped in incognito to do two things, To visit you and to lay wreaths On the grave of my son Edward. How well are you playing your role as the vanguard Of your people in the march towards emancipation From oppressors and degradation That all people of Africa Suffer since the days some of them were shipped to America?
Chilembwe	Our sufferings have multiplied Since you departed from this country. Now I am disappointed Of ever regaining our rights, human and political, I have petitioned Government officials and have been rebuffed by them all.
Booth	Elaborate on that so I may know where things stand In this beautiful country called Nyasaland.
Chilembwe	Wherever we blacks go we are insulted. White farmers and traders say each of us is a bastard. Nay, they call us, niggers and other contemptible Names; for us to live happily here has become impossible.
Booth	About the position of the African tenant Has there been any improvement?
Chilembwe	Not at all, the situation has become worse If the Hebrews' suffering was harsh in Egypt, ours is a curse. The *thangata* system has reduced us blacks into servitude, I wonder where is British gratitude To us Nyasa people for the blood and sweat We have sacrificed in extending the British Empire in Africa east and west? Behold right now Residents are forcing African people To go north and fight in a war that is most horrible. From battlefields in German East Africa most of my people never come back

	They are seized, maimed, killed by General Lettow von Vorbeck. Now tell me, Reverend Booth, shall we Africans be better treated once This great war is over and belligerent nations have signed the armistice?
Booth	The white man won't treat you any better; He will continue to treat his dogs dearer To him than his native servant. Your agonies will not diminish but grow rampant Unless you, John, assume the role of Moses And lead your people out of this land of abuses.
Chilembwe	But, how? What can I do?
Booth	Moses had Canaan to take his people to, Because his people in Egypt were strangers not Egyptian. But Africa is for the African, Just as America is for the American. It is your oppressor that must quit and go. If he cannot be persuaded to depart, strike him with a blow.
Chilembwe	But, but, ba
Booth	Ah, like Moses you are stammering; Like the Hebrew leader you are trembling. When the Lord commands you to save your people from bondage. Just summon up a bit of your courage God took Moses through, He will do the same to you.
Chilembwe	Well,-eh,-well- *(Feeling being shaken up)*
Ida	Wake up darling. The sun is already up in the morning, The water is ready in the bathroom.
Chilembwe	Ah, so this is just a dream. Perhaps I should forget it, but can I?

Ida	What did you dream that makes you sigh?
Chilembwe	In my dream I was by the River Mbombwe, When I heard someone calling Chilembwe, Chilembwe. He brought me a message from God. I am Black Moses, so I was told. I must lead my people to freedom, Away from the life of *thangata* serfdom, Oppression in this country must go By any means, even by a mighty blow.
Ida	Why do you bother yourself so much With problems that are such As do not burden us alone. About these problems, as I see them, nothing can be done. With us life is not very tough. Our wardrobe is full, so is our granary. About certain problems let's not worry. But just go on providing our people with education And spreading the Christian religion. Please, please, John, give up the politics. They bite more than deadly ticks.
Chilembwe	That may be so, Ida, my darling But I feel I must act boldly against those who are troubling Us sons and daughters of Africa. I must put into practice ideas I learned in America.
Ida	What are those ideas, may I know Them; are they wise, tell me yes or no?
Chilembwe	In due course I will tell you everything, For the time being just be patient, darling, I must first discuss the grand ideas with a few Of my friends. Others will know when time is due.
Ida	The more you say that The more you whet my appetite; Like any woman, curiosity is either my strength or weakness. When you withhold from me some secrets You deprive me of happiness.

Chilembwe	Oh, darling, what has been started under the sun cannot be concealed forever.
Time will come when I will whisper
To you the essence of my grand enterprise.
Meanwhile, as usual, I beseech you, support me with prayers.
By the way, where is Wilfred Mtambo?
I want also, Chigamba, Jamali and Isaac Chambo
To go and summon my henchmen here.
Ida	They are in our field cultivating. Let me go and call them for you, my dear.
Meanwhile get on with your breakfast.
Chilembwe	Thank you my dearest.
(The young men walk in)
Young men, for now lay down your axes and hoes,
With the speed of the evening swallows.
You Chambo go and call the Mkulichi brothers, Steven and Andrew.
You Pilgrim Chigamba go to Migowi where you grew
Up and call your uncle Kaduya, David,
But not his brother Garnet
Whom I do not very much trust.
Garnet Kaduya is not very much of a patriot,
As for you, Jamali, go and fetch
Duncan Njilima. He knows much
That we shall find useful
In the struggle against foreign rule.
Wilfred Mtambo, looking tall and slim,
With the speed of a cheetah go and call him,
I mean the most talented of my colleagues, John Grey Kufa.
And on your way back hand this letter to Cedrick Chikafa.
(Turning to his wife)
Mother of John Junior.
Ida	Yes, Father of John Junior
Chilembwe	Give the young men cups of tea and pieces of bread, because
Hungry people do not serve well a worthy cause.

Ida	With pleasure that I'll do. *(After the messengers have departed)* So you have sent for Kufa too?
Chilembwe	Yes, of course. Is he unwell?
Ida	With him life is a bit of hell. Of late he has become suspicious of his wife. Between him and her there is constant strife.
Chilembwe	Really, tell me that which I don't know And why the couple's life should be so.
Ida	As many people say, we women love to talk In order to kill the boredom of idleness or kitchen work. Whether we are two or in a bigger group, We may be reluctant to share salt or soup, But we readily share things that are dearer in our lives, I mean stories about quarrelling husbands and wives. At last week's meeting of the sewing class Mrs. Mbendera talked about her husband's waywardness, She asked us what she should do about it? Mrs. Kufa said "Revenge, and why not". She was adamant with her opinion That a woman should pay a wayward husband in the coin. Since then I understand she's putting her ideas into practice; Of her movements, Mr. Kufa has become suspicious.
Chilembwe	That's very sad.
Ida	And very bad.
Chilembwe	If only I could help them reconcile, I would do this as soon as possible. But in marriage affairs we make things worse Through intervention, we simply achieve the reverse. Since Kufa has kept his worries secret I will do nothing but keep quiet.
Ida	I agree with you, We have so much to do. It's better to leave certain things alone. And now it's time I go back to the kitchen.
Chilembwe	And I must go to the New Jerusalem Church.

Scene II

In the New Jerusalem Church

Chilembwe, Kaduya, Zimba, Mkulichi brothers, Njilima, Mtambo, Kufa

Chilembwe	We are all in except John Grey, He is usually punctual, why not today?
Stephen Mkulichi	Perhaps he has another row with his wife, These days Kufa lives a miserable life.
Chilembwe	It's sad to hear that.
Zimba	Sad indeed, especially when you witness How they shout at each other abuses and curses.
Kaduya	He was usually regarded as a happily married man, What has happened to the couple, under the sun?
Zimba	I don't know for sure, But I understand a third man with motives that are impure Has deflected Mrs. Kufa's heart from her husband, The ravisher dwells on Kufa's own land.
Mkulichi	That's what I have learned from my own wife, Kufa the intellectual no longer leads a happy life.
Zimba	So our wives are sources of news.
Mkulichi	About domestic secrets a wife knows A good deal more than a husband, For women talk and talk when they pound maize in…
Kaduya	Kufa is too soft, Why does he not Kill the snatcher? And why spare the wife Who exposes him to danger?
Mkulichi	Kill one's wife and her lover! That would be going too far.
Kaduya	That's the solution when …
Zimba	Shoo- let's be talking about the weather. See, Kufa is just coming up there.

Chilembwe	Welcome John Grey, please do Come in. We could not start the meeting without you. Where a problem requires intellect Your contribution is at its best.
Kufa	For coming so late, I am sorry, I was trying to sort out certain things that give me a bit of worry.
Chilembwe	Better late than absent. Now, compatriots, with your consent, Let me begin the meeting with a prayer. *Almighty God in heaven up there,* *Jesus said we should seek your kingdom* *First. This we have done, now Lord give us freedom* *From those who are in Africa to oppress us,* *Those who have deprived Nyasa people of their happiness.* *In Christ's name we pray thee. Amen.*
All	Amen.
Chilembwe	You will remember two months ago I went to Chiradzulu *boma* and saw Mitchell the Resident About the various types of mistreatment That our people suffer on private estates, The sufferings which have grown since I returned from the United States. I spoke about the injustice of taxation Without any kind of representation; And against the holding of married women As hostages while their men Go about trying to find the tax money. I spoke about every problem. To all these issues Mitchell replied that we black people behave like our so-called ancestor Ham.
Kaduya	The devil how could he abuse us like that? Had I been there I would have beaten him right on the spot.
Chilembwe	No doubt you would have done what you say;

However we are here to discuss the more appropriate day
When to start an action
That will lead us to freedom and liberation.
Hence I put before you all
Africa's great call
To its brave sons to get freedom
And do away with *thangata* serfdom.
When I was in America I listened to two great Black voices,
I listened to Booker Washington and Dr Dubois.
Washington said if we Blacks are to be respected by white people
We must be more practical;
One farm well kept, one large house bought,
One school building or church well kept,
One man an honest and regular tax payer,
One patient cured by a black doctor,
These would earn the black man the white man's respect,
The white man would no longer treat us with contempt,
Now he would extend to us blacks fraternity and equality.
But for the past fourteen years, have we not made the PIM a model community
Where men and women work hard and dress smartly,
Where the compound is green and kept neatly?
White people still call us apes, niggers, other names of contempt,
We have reached a stage
When it's not enough to whine or rage,
No more mere talking,
There must be fighting.
May I ask each of you which is better, to be a brave patriot or to be a coward?

All   Spit on the coward.

Chilembwe   You have answered well.
Foreigners have turned our land into hell.
Active resistance is what Dubois advocated.
Sooner or later to get Africa liberated'
We must adopt the only method that can work.
They have called us dogs, let's bite, not just bark.

	Let's recall how George Washington fought
	And set his country free, a lesson to us well-taught.
	Toussaint liberated his country Haiti
	When Napoleon Bonaparte
	Was fighting the British people.
	Now the British are fighting the German people,
	Let's take up arms and strike a blow
	From which slavery will die, freedom will grow.
Zimba	Eh, listen what is that?
Mkulichi	What is the noise about?
Kufa	*(Standing up)* It is the newly recruited soldiers,
	On the march doing exercise.
	They do this day and night,
	Preparing to go north and fight
	Soldiers of the German Kaiser
	Who threatens the British Empire.
	(They all listen to the soldiers' song)
	Chorus
	Young men of Nyasaland march on; left, right, left, right,
	Northward we must go and fight,
	The Kaiser, the German devil,
	We shall fight and fight till
	Our King George, the Emperor,
	Seizes German colonies and rules everywhere.
Chilembwe	Tut, tut, there our people go to fight for a cause
	None of them really knows.
	They will endure hardships of every kind,
	Thirst, hunger, death, leaving behind
	Orphans and widows doing *thangata* work
	On the white man's farm from dawn to dusk.
	Let us get back our freedom now,
	And not waste time asking how.
Kaduya	I fought for the British
	In Somaliland. Later they dumped me like rubbish.
	Major Henderson who was with me now owns thousands
	Of acres of land that belonged to my ancestors.
	It's time to fight for our country.

	It's not enough just to be angry.
	When our petitions they ignore,
	What is stolen from us we must restore.
Kufa	But can we win the battle for freedom?
	Are we not heading for doom,
	Fighting a war without up-to date weapons?
Njilima	I see that Kufa has a point.
Kaduya	You, Njilima, you are also a coward.
	Remember whether you fight or not, one day you will be dead.
Chilembwe	Well, dear compatriots, let's not exchange abuses,
	Nor engage in excuses
	For not doing what must be done,
	At all costs freedom must be won.
	Those who seek freedom and justice God shows them the light.
	As we go marching on the battlefield, let us sing, "In God we trust."
	The hour of freedom is now, now.
All	Nau, Nau.
Chilembwe	Njilima, you have said
	We must have plans well laid.
	I can assure you, dear compatriot,
	I have already given the plans serious thought.
	The first thing we should do to achieve our freedom
	Is to go about talking to people, those of them
	That have great grievances.
	Among these are the chiefs whom the foreign rulers
	Have demoted to glorified messengers.
	We must go and tell them they will regain authority,
	Have wealth befitting royalty,
	If they support us in this endeavour
	Whose goal is freedom and black power.
Mkulichi	Just a moment, Reverend Pastor,
	There is noise once more coming from outside there.
Chilembwe	Again go and find out

What it is all about.
(They listen)

Chorus

Amayi ndi Abambo, tsalani.	Mothers and fathers, stay well.
Abale ndi alongo, tsalani.	Brothers and sisters, stay well.
Ife tikupita ku nkhondo	We are going to war
Kukamenyana ndi a Kaizara	To fight the Kaiser
Amene asowetsa mtendere anthu.	Who has put mankind's freedom in danger.
Amayi ndi Abambo,	Mothers and fathers,
abale ndi alongo, tsalani.	Bothers and sisters, stay well.
Zikayenda bwino tikabwerako	We may return if all goes well.
Koma Mulungu akanena	If God decides otherwise
tidzaonana kumwamba.	We will meet in heaven.
Tikumbukireni mu mapemphero.	Do pray for us your children.

Mkulichi More recruits for the King's African Rifles,
Going to Karonga to die on the white man's battlefields.

Chilembwe That makes my heart boil,
They are taking sons of this soil
To go and fight in the so-called civilized man's wars,
To die there, leaving widows and children with sorrows,
If our soldiers have to fight, then they must fight
For justice, land and the right
To determine what is good for themselves,
To live as free men, rather than die as slaves.
You are raising your hand Kaduya,
Speak, Alleluia.

All Amen.

Kaduya I know most leading soldiers in the KAR]
I was with them in Somaliland and elsewhere.
I will go and persuade them
To join the war for African Freedom.
I also know the chiefs quite well,
All those that in valleys and on hills do dwell.
I will easily persuade them to fight for the grand
Cause of our beautiful Nyasaland.

Chilembwe Kaduya you deserve the name David
For you resemble the King of Judah out and out.

	There will come a day
	When people will sing and say
	"Here was a man who toiled and sweated for this country's freedom
	Now he must be with angels up there in God's kingdom."
	Any more volunteers?
Njilima	I will contact *boma* messengers
	And tell them once independence is won
	They will become district commissioners.
Chilembwe	Good, John Grey Kufa, our great intellectual,
	Let's have a piece of your wisdom as usual.
Kufa	I will recruit the Lomwe toilers on estates here and there,
	In bravery they have no superior.
Chilembwe	As for me, I will concentrate on Nyasa followers
	Or adherents of other churches.
	I will invite them to join us in the quest
	For liberty, equality and fraternity.
	Time has come for the oppressor to die or go.
	No more talking, let's strike the blow!
	But before we depart let's pray.
	Lord up in Heaven, this day
	We have started a brave act.
	We beseech thee to bless it.
	Be with us as you were with the people of Haiti
	When they threw up the tyranny of Bonaparte;
	We too have a cause that deserves to be won.
	We have already sought and found thy kingdom.
	To it, Lord, may you add our earthly freedom.
	In Jesus name,
	Here we come.
	Amen.
All	Amen, amen.

Scene III

Chilembwe, Joseph Bismarck at Bismarck's farm

Bismarck	Good afternoon, Pastor.
Chilembwe	Good afternoon, my dear brother
Bismarck	It is a long time you last left PIM by the River Mbombwe To visit us; is there something special, Rev. Chilembwe? Maybe you are bringing us good news, Perhaps bad news, who knows.
Chilembwe	I bring no news that would cause fear. Peace be to you and your dear Ones. True, I have come on serious business, But it all has to do with our lost happiness.
Bismarck	But how have you left the family?
Chilembwe	My wife Ida is joyfully teaching her fellow women How to groom themselves and care for their children. She sends her greetings to Mrs. Bismarck And hopes, your lady too enjoys her work.
Bismarck	Why then did you not bring with you Mrs. Chilembwe and the young ones too? It's high time our two families Chatted and saw each other more often these days.
Chilembwe	One day I will do as you suggest, But today I thought it best To come and see you all by myself. Can we walk into the centre of your farm, There to talk without causing alarm? By chance, have your farm workers gone home? For the time being I don't want them To hear what I am going to say, Though hear of it they must one day.
Bismarck	Most of them have gone home already, On Saturday I allow them to leave by midday, Unlike the white estate managers Who make the people do *thangata* work Six days a week from dawn to dusk.
Chilembwe	Ah, *thangata* is what I have come to talk about,

	The system that has turned our people into serfs out and out.
Bismarck	Let's go behind that anthill, Where the grass and shrubs will conceal us well.
Chilembwe	*(Casting eyes far up).* Have a look at Mount Soche there, And at Mount Mulanje; beauty, beauty everywhere, And yet we can no longer enjoy these natural gifts at all. God created us free, but we are now slaves of other people. Foreigners call us by names most contemptible; Nigger, Kaffir, native, bloody fool. Have you ever thought of doing something about these things, brother, Or are you one of those who do not bother?
Bismarck	You have reminded me of a painful incident in my life. Two months ago I was almost involved in a fateful strife, With a whiteman called Mario Blanco. He works for Conforzi Estates in Thyolo. "Take off your hat," he shouted at me, His voice sounded like that of a bumble bee. "Come on, ape, I am talking to you. I replied, "I am not an ape but a human being like you." He drew his revolver Mumbling "fiddle de dee". He was about to shoot me When my wife took the hat off my head To save me from being shot dead. "Oh, so your head has less hair than an egg," he said. I walked away feeling pain from legs to the head.
Chilembwe	You have then been insulted by crude white people.
Bismarck	More times than I can recall. One called me Joseph Pumpkin In front of my kith and kin.
Chilembwe	What do you intend to do with these abuses, Just sit and watch them get worse?
Bismarck	What else can I do? If there is a solution let me know from you.

Chilembwe	Bad whites must go back home. This man Mario Bianco must go back to Rome. William Livingstone, back to Scotland, We don't want such people in Nyasaland.
Bismarck	By what means can you force them home, Chilembwe? Have you got policeman and soldiers there by the River Mbombwe?
Chilembwe	This is precisely why I've come Here to talk about raising a freedom Army among those who work for you, And this job you can help me to do.
Bismarck	I have always appreciated what you say, But not what you are talking about today.
Chilembwe	I speak of African freedom, Getting rid of slavery and serfdom; To be free we must strike a blow. And force the oppressors to go.
Bismarck	Perhaps you are tired of life, Why engage in a kind of strife That will ruin you and your family. I plead with you solemnly To give up this dangerous thought. It will make you lose a lot. You might be jailed, You might be killed.
Chilembwe	Whoever is born today, poor or rich, Must sooner or later perish. The name of whosoever dies while serving his people Will last; it may not die at all.
Bismarck	That might be so, pastor, But what I know is that whenever Black people have revolted against white men's rule, White armies have defeated them for sure. The Black man's life has then become worse not better This happened in the war of Kibiliti in Mozambique up there.

	In 1904 the Zulu revolted, led by Bambata,
	They were crushed, now they suffer a worse form of *thangata*.
	Revolts bring floods of tears and blood, this much you know,
	To your appeals I definitely say no-no.
Chilembwe	Oh, dear, if that's so, alas,
	You will not be numbered with those of us
	Who will risk our lives for this country.
	In cowardice there is shame, in bravery there's glory.
Bismarck	Do you mean you have spoken to many other people
	And without hesitation they all
	Have agreed to follow you on this road,
	Which you should not take, being a man of God?
Chilembwe	I and my henchmen have spoken to many more people than I can remember.
	We have recruits in Chiradzulu here, in Mulanje up there
	In Ntcheu my lieutenant is Philip Chinyama,
	In Dowa there is Pastor Ndalama
	Who is talking to chief Chiwere.
	In Zomba there is Simon Kadewere.
	All these have agreed to follow me
	In the struggle to get ourselves free.
Bismarck-	For the moment I withdraw the word, no,
	This much you may wish to know,
	Though in my mind there's lingering doubt,
	I will give the matter a more serious thought.
Chilembwe	May I ask you not to talk about
	To those who can betray us.
Bismarck	I swear by God's Book of truth,
	I am no blabbermouth.

Scene IV

Chilembwe, Kundecha by River Domasi

Kundecha	Welcome, Pastor John Chilembwe, It's a long way from the River Mbombwe And yet you have decided to visit us here by the River Domasi
Chilembwe	Yes, having visited a friend at Naisi, I said why not visit an even dearer friend, Reverend Kundecha. Sorry I did not send Advance notice of my coming.
Kundecha	Never mind, so how is everything With you, pastor?
Chilembwe	Now I am out of danger of the asthma attack And the little ache on my back. I hope you too are well.
Kundecha	For me last week my health was just hell, I had an acute attack of malaria. By God's mercy I have recovered and once more sing alleluia, With regained energy I carry on God's work Visiting the healthy ones, comforting the sick. *(Enters Mrs. Kundecha)*
Mrs. Kundecha	Welcome to tea, pastor, Here are scones and there's butter.
Chilembwe	Thanks, these are nice scones, Madam.
Mrs. Kundecha	Would you like to have them with jam?
Chilembwe	No, thanks *(Mrs. Kundecha departs)* Brother, why don't you buy your wife dresses That would make her look a lady of modern times.
Kundecha	Is she not well dressed, pastor?
Chilembwe	I feel that the wife of a pastor And that of any educated person Should be up-to-date in dress every season.
Kundecha	With the meagre salary of a pastor, How can I dress my wife any better?
Chilembwe	Ida my wife is a good tailor,

	I suggest you advise Mrs. Kundecha to visit her. Ida has made fine frocks out of material That does not cost me a good deal. *(A little girl called Dalitso walks in looking pregnant)*
Dalitso	Good afternoon, pastor. Here is a letter from my father. Stay well.
Kundecha	Go well. *(Girl exits)*
Chilembwe	To me that girl looks as if soon she will be a mother.
Kundecha	She has married a man as old as her father.
Chilembwe	Oh God, she's too young to be a wife, At her age she should have an easier life Than shouldering the burden of pregnancy and motherhood. Child marriages must stop, they are not good.
Kundecha	Pastor, it's the custom of our ancestors For parents to hand their daughters In marriages when still young and unspoiled By too many things that get girl's soiled.
Chilembwe	This custom retards our progress in modern civilization, We can give it up through education. Parents should not only send their daughters To school, but keep them there as long as they keep the sons. Educate a man, you educate one person only, Educate a woman, you educate a family. We Africans won't find the right position in the international community Until we concede to our women folk equality.
Kundecha	You seem to have learned these ideas in America, They are rather too modern for us in Africa. We believe women must cook and bear children, It's not yet time to talk of equality between men, women.

Chilembwe	There's something else about which I would like to speak to you That I learned in America too. But I would like to do so while gazing at Zomba mountain, Beautiful mountains refresh my brain. *(They go outside)* Behold the beauties of our mountains, behold the green vegetation and the rivers. Prophet Isaiah was right: How lovely on the mountains are the feet That proclaim the tidings of deliverance.
Kundecha	Zomba mountain inspires me as I go round Preaching God's holiness all over the land And Christ's readiness to receive those who repent, Give up sinful ways and dwell in God's holy tent.
Chilembwe	Having preached of sin and repentance, What else do you do to advance The well-being of our people?
Kundecha	I am called to spread the word of God, that's all.
Chilembwe	When our Lord Jesus started his mission In Nazareth, he promised redemption To those who were living as captives. Are you happy that colonial settlers call us bloody natives?
Kundecha	The word of God that I preach to the people Releases them from the grip of the Devil.
Chilembwe	That's a limited view, I would advise you To read St John chapter eight, verse Thirty two, what Jesus Said when he was in Galilee That truth shall make us free. We are people living in a house of bondage, No matter how well educated he may be, to white people a black man is just a savage. And yet right now they are forcing our people to go out and fight the Kaiser, Paying them peanuts while exposing them to grave danger.

Kundecha	What you say sounds true and clear, But what can we do about such things, oh dear?
Chilembwe	We at the PIM have hatched a plan That will set free every man and woman. I have come here to seek your cooperation In the struggle to end our oppression, To set up our own government; The hour of political redemption is imminent. Preach this to such of your congregation As can be trusted to join the struggle for liberation. Persuade them to join us on the day of the uprising This will be the day the British and the Germans are busy fighting.
Kundecha	You surprise me, Reverend Chilembwe, After baptizing people in the River Mbombwe Proclaiming peace to all people of goodwill, How can you advocate war, it's so evil?
Chilembwe	When faced by tyrants as cruel as The marauding beast, one has No option but fight them with a gun. In this way was independence in America and Haiti won.
Kundecha	Your thoughts have taken you too far. Go back and seek God's guidance, pastor, Retrace your steps, tread on the holy path. Where you are heading now there's no salvation but miserable death, Not only for you, But your beloved loved ones too.
Chilembwe	To die in the course of liberating one's people Is a task most noble. Kundecha, my friend, let's join hands, make our people free. They will then sing hymns with the melody of that bird in the tree.
Kundecha	Give me time to seek guidance from the Lord, Whether it's meet that I participate in an act so bold.

Chilembwe	I will not waste more of your time, brother, But only this I must ask you, pastor. Not to talk to anyone about These things until you are no longer in doubt That it is sinless to fight for a national cause. Cowardly people might betray us, who knows.
Kundecha	Trust me to keep it a secret.
Chilembwe	That's perfect. Now, brother stay well.
Kundecha	Go well.

Scene V

Kaduya, Masangano, Mitundu

Masangano	Ah, there you come, famous David Kaduya, At last you have visited me, alleluia. You are most welcome. How have you left home?
Kaduya	Everybody at home is okay. I have decided to visit you today To partake of the big harvest You have got from this estate.
Masangano	Oh, my friend, are you laughing at me? Can't you see that all I have is an acre. The rest of my father's land in now over there.
Kaduya	Where?
Masangano	It is part of the Bruce Estates.
Kaduya	So you too have been dispossessed of your acres of land?
Masangano	All that I till is a patch of sand.
Kaduya	Well, can we go inside the house if you don't mind, John Chilembwe has sent me to deliver to you a message of the most confidential kind.

Masangano	Let's go into the house of my friend Mitumba, In my house there are visitors from Zomba.
	(Inside Mitumba's house)
Kaduya	What book is this?
Masangano	It is the Bible, of course.
Kaduya	Open Isaiah chapter fifty-two and then Read verses one to seven.
Masangano	*(Reading)* Awake, awake! Put on strength, O Zion; Put on beautiful garments, O Jerusalem, the holy city, For there shall no more come Into you the uncircumcised and the unclean. Shake yourself from the dust, arise, O captive Jerusalem, Loose the bonds from your neck, O captive daughter of Zion. For thus says the Lord. "You were sold for nothing, and you shall be redeemed without money."
Kaduya	What do you understand by the works 'Awake, awake'?
Masangano	They mean that for Christ's sake We should be alert of the devil In case he tempts us to do evil.
Kaduya	Oh, George Masangano, you are slumbering While foreigners are plundering The land God gave our ancestors. The passage means all the nations Must fight for their freedom, Have their own flag and kingdom. Jesus came to liberate Jews from Roman rule But of his mission the Jews were not sure. They handed him to Pontius Pilate who hanged him on a tree. They lost a golden opportunity. To this day they are not free.

Masangano	That's strange for me to hear.
	I don't understand; make it clear.
Kaduya	Truth shall make us free and glorious,
	If we follow the one God has sent us.
	The Almighty has sent to Nyasas John Chilembwe
	Who, having baptized people with water in the River Mbombwe,
	Is now set to baptize them with the spirit of freedom,
	That will remove the curse of slavery and serfdom,
	Behold, countrymen, the world is coming to an end.
	Once more God is going to send
	Floods to punish sinners and oppressors as in the days of Noah.
	Some will perish by the sword like King Saul at Gilboa.
	But they will be safe and sound those people
	Who will respond to Chilembwe's clarion call.
	And stand up for freedom.
	Those who hesitate or refuse will face doom.
Masangano	How can we be sure of what you say
	In this month of February and on a cloudy day?
Kaduya	An angel of God visited Chilembwe
	By the River Mbombwe,
	While he was baptizing,
	And told him God had been listening
	To the wailing of the Black people in Africa
	As well as those in America.
	To each nation God has sent a liberator.
	For us Nyassa, Chilembwe is our God-given leader.
Masangano	That sounds strange to me.
Kaduya	There will be many strange things to see
	During this year of nineteen fourteen
	As it comes to an end giving way to nineteen fifteen.
	John Chilembwe is going to clear out.
	Land grabbers and oppressors; about this have no doubt.
	The hour of redemption is at hand.
	We will regain our liberty and our land.

Mitumba	But can we fight white men, Without guns and hope to win?
Kaduya	We will fight with a variety of weapons Such as poisoned arrows and sharpened spears; We will have plenty of guns too. What I say is not false but true. Don't fear the white man's gun powder. When enemy bullets touch our bodies they will turn into water. Chief Gulugufe has within his domain A man called Udabwe, a super-magician. On the battle field that day Gulugufe and Udabwe, will scatter pieces of wood and pebbles of clay. As the enemy soldiers come marching towards us Behind them they will be attacked by lions and snakes. Some will be gored by buffaloes While we release on them bullets and arrows. We will fight courageously, we will win. The Lord above will proclaim Chilembwe our King Those who will be against him shall perish. To *thangata* tenants Chilembwe will restore land, Everybody will be happier in Nyasaland.
Mitumba	What about you, Will you become a ruler too?
Kaduya	Mine are humble ambitions, To be appointed simply a director of deportations; My job will be to deport from our country The bad foreigners, all and sundry. Come forward, countrymen, join the army of liberation, There will be victory, followed by jubilation.
Masangano	Well, Mitumba, you have heard What Kaduya has said, Do you have any comment to make?
Mitumba	Of course; for goodness sake We must go where Chilembwe will go. The time has come to strike a blow

	On those who trample on us.
	God will give us victory most glorious.
Kaduya	That's beautifully said, Mitumba,
	Chilembwe will make you mayor of Zomba.
	What about you, Masangano, what do you say?
	What will you be doing on the liberation day?
Masangano	I will be fighting along the rest
	With vim, vigour and zest.
Kaduya	Good. Now comrades, let's recite this oath,
	That will strengthen the faith,
	Which will make us fight till victory
	Shines on our faces and we free our country.
	(Kaduya reads the oath, Masangano and Mitumba repeat)
	I believe in Chilembwe the leader
	Whom God has given to us as the Redeemer,
	And I believe he will do to Nyasaland what George Washington did to America
	For he is the blessed son of Africa.
	The day he blows the trumpet
	Calling me to the battlefield, I will go and fight,
	For freedom
	That will end *thangata* serfdom.
	But if I refuse to go,
	And take part in striking the freedom blow,
	Or if before that day,
	I stupidly betray
	Chilembwe as Judas Iscariot
	Did to Jesus Christ,
	May this oath kill me.
	God bless Africa, make us free.
	(Kaduya departs)

Scene VI

Mitchell, Mandota, Mwenye, Morrison

Mitchell	I have received this note from Bishop Auneau. By any chance do you know A man called Morrison Chilembwe?
Mandota	He is a nephew of John Chilembwe. That day when Chilembwe came to see you Morrison accompanied him too.
Mitchell	Go and bring him here, Apparently he has a story worthy of my ear. *(Enters Morrison)*
Mitchell	Are you Morrison?
Morrison	I am the one.
Mitchell	Do you know this man? *(pointing at Paul Mwenye)*
Morrison	No, I don't know him
Mitchell	Is this man the Morrison you were talking about? *(Facing Mwenyu)*
Paul Mwenye	I think so, I have no doubt.
Mitchell	I have got a report That John Chilembwe is scheming a plot To kill white men, women and children, Take over the government and establish his barbaric reign Of terror. Such information I understand you gave to this man Paul.
Morrison	As I have said I don't know this man at all; Moreover, what he said to you about John Chilembwe is a lie with a capital L; The lie that will take this man to hell. My uncle John Chilembwe is a man of peace. At no time has he harboured an evil thought about people of any race.
Mitchell	Look here, native, if you tell the truth, You will get a reward that's worth Much more than you earn per year.
Morrison	What more can I say, oh dear? There is no other truth than that which I have given.

	My uncle is a holy man of God, not a murderous heathen.
	Daily he talks of love and kindness.
	Whoever accuses him of murderous intents is suffering from madness.

| Mitchell | But why should this man from Nguludi tell a lie about you? |

Morrison	This lie must have something to do
	With what you and I know
	About that missionary at Nguludi, Bishop Auneau;
	He hates Chilembwe, regards him a competitor
	For schools. Sir, don't believe this man
	Here, he is just a weapon of someone who wants to destroy the Providence Industrial Mission.

| Mitchell | Paul, this man is denying what you told Bishop Auneau, |
| | Tell me more about what you yourself know. |

P. Mwenye	Should I have to swear by Mother Maria
	In whom I believe and sing alleluia?
	But the Decalogue says don't bear false witness
	Against anyone. To do so is sinfulness.

Mitchell	I don't want to hear homilies.
	Just tell me the truth, not lies.
	Who told you that John Chilembwe plots to kill white people?
	Answer this in a manner plain and simple.

Mwenye	I know, but don't know enough.
	What I say may sound like a bluff.
	Well, well, Morrison ah yes, Morrison told me something- ho, ho, ho,
	But I do remember something oh, no, no, no.

| Mitchell | Be direct man, pin this man down, |
| | Stop behaving like a clown. |

Morrison	Sir, something is wrong with this man's head;
	The truth is what I have said.
	Chilembwe is faithful to God and loyal to the government.
	Besides educating and converting people to Christianity, Chilembwe has no other intent.

Mitchell	Morrison, I see some truth in what you say. Go back home and have a good day.
Mwenye	May I also go back to my drink? It would be nice, I think.
Mitchell	No, *(turning to Mandota)* take him to the cell, But look after him well.

Scene VII

Hetherwick, Kundecha, Matecheta Bismarck at Henry Henderson Institute

Hetherwick	Welcome, brothers in Christ. Let's first have a short prayer before we start; *Our heavenly father we come before thee* *That you may help us to see* *And behold the truth that's hidden* *From us, for we are but your children.* *Let our tongues speak to each other nothing but the truth* *In the name of Jesus Christ, founder of our faith,* *We pray* *And say*
All	Amen.
Hetherwick	I have detained you after today's Kirk Session in case you can help me answer this letter from the Resident It says John Chilembwe is plotting a rising against the government. Has anyone of you ever heard such a rumour?
Bismarck	From whom did the Resident get the rumour?
Hetherwick	From his assistant Phillip Mitchell, Whom you all know very well.
Bismarck	I have heard some men saying God is soon to send Floods to put the world to an end, That those who don't follow Chilembwe will drown While Jesus will come and put a crown On Chilembwe's head,

	Judge the living and the dead.
	But when I was with Chilembwe recently,
	Of these things he himself said nothing absolutely.
Hetherwick	Where did you meet him?
Bismarck	Near my farm, he was just passing by
	He stopped, spoke to me briefly and said goodbye.
Hetherwick	What did he say
	By the way?
Bismarck	He congratulated me regarding my crops and livestock.
	He then went on with vehemence to talk
	As he usually does against the early marriage of girls.
	He said they should remain in school as long as the boys;
	In this way Nyasaland will grow faster in modern civilization
	And that eventually we shall become a worthy nation.
Kundecha	Chilembwe said the same thing to me about girls education.
Hetherwick	Did he say something else to you, Steven?
Kundecha	Three weeks ago he stopped at my house for a while,
	He talked about dressing African wives in modern style.
	He spoke of nothing else that day.
	This is all I wanted to say.
Hetherwick	And you, Harry?
Matecheta	I slept at Chilembwe's mission two months ago;
	I didn't enjoy my sleep, oh no;
	His people forced me to keep listening
	To their endless grumbling.
Hetherwick	What did they grumble about?
Matecheta	They talked about the treatment they get
	From the Resident and Mr. Bruce
	As well as Bruce's farm managers at his estate.
	They said these white men burn PIM prayer houses
	And forbid Chilembwe to open schools
	At Magomero. They spoke against *thangata*, labour rent.

	They also grumbled about mainstream missionaries and the Government
	I urged them to trust in God
	Who in the fullness of time would
	Bring about mutual understanding between races of mankind.
	Then they said, let us read to you a Bible passage if you don't mind,
	They read in John chapter eight; *truth shall make you free.*
	Then they stared at me.
	But by this time I was dozing
	And had given up listening.
Kundecha	Oh, yes, I remember, Chilembwe also spoke to me,
	About truth making people free.
	To this verse he attached a meaning of his own,
	But he did not say anything about starting a rebellion.
Hetherwick	Now I ask all of you
	This little task to do.
	As you go about visiting parishes,
	Teaching and preaching in prayer houses,
	Within Chiradzulu sub district especially,
	About Chilembwe's clandestine doings enquire cautiously,
	I myself very much doubt
	That Chilembwe would be so foolish as to start a revolt.
	However, where there's smoke there could be fire.
	So gently go about listening to what people are saying here and there.
	(Exit Hetherwick)
	(Bismarck, Matecheta and Kundecha alone depart together)
Bismarck	I am coming out of this meeting rather uneasy,
	My conscience is not clear but hazy.
Kundecha	Why?
Bismarck	I have denied the truth that I know.
	Chilembwe did come to me and talked about striking a blow.
	Against foreign rulers and oppressors.

	He appealed to me to help him recruit volunteers. I refused, but promised not to betray Him. That's why today, Rather than betray a friend, I have told a lie befitting of a fiend.
Kundecha	He said the same thing to me, So we are in the same boat, I can see. Rather than betray our compatriot Let's just by prayer persuade him not To do that which is evil. How can the hand that baptizes also kill?
Matecheta	I agree with you. Let's go home and pray That God's love should grow in Chilembwe's heart from day to day.
All	Amen.

Act Four

Scene I

Chilembwe, Kaduya, Zimba, Kufa, Njilima, Matola, in the church

Chilembwe	Greetings to you all, freedom fighter and seekers of dignity.
All	And to you, our leader, given to us by the Almighty.
Chilembwe	All these months we've been talking About the day we would go fighting For the liberation of our country. We have so far not fixed the day To start, but this much I can say. It seems we are too late for action, But on this I must seek your opinion
Kaduya	An opinion I will venture to give, pastor. But what is in that piece of paper?

Chilembwe	This is a letter from Chikwana Moses. You know him. He works in the Chief Secretary's office. I will read it.
Kaduya	Let us listen, you there be quiet.
Chilembwe	(Reading) A week ago you received a letter from the Secretary For Native affairs, saying He would come and visit you To discuss the problems you Had raised in the *Nyasaland Times*. He is to bring with Him soldiers and policemen To arrest you. They will pretend to Take you to Mauritius. At the sea They will throw you Overboard and then say You jumped into it yourself in trying to escape. The rest of us they Will shoot in cold blood Or drag us to the army, To the front line and get us Killed by Lettow von Vorbeck's German soldiers. All this is contained In their secret documents, Which I have come across By chance. Quickly Therefore, God-given leader Decide whether to fight or to flee.
Kufa	Let us flee.
Kaduya	That won't make us free. To run away from a worthy cause is childish. There is no going back, let us go and fight the British
Kufa	Those who are poorly prepared for a battle field Risk being heavily defeated.
Kaduya	I got pledges of support from all the chiefs. And some members of the King's African Rifles,

	Oh, pastor Chilembwe, God-anointed leader, command me, I will obey. I can start the fight even today.
Njilima	I agree with Kaduya out and out, That we are fully prepared for the fight, there's no doubt. In Blantyre government messengers, clerks, watchmen are waiting To hear the trumpet's sound; they will come out fighting. Comrades, don't listen to Kufa; though he is bright, What he says is not always right.
Chilembwe	Well, Kufa, John Gray, Tomorrow is the day The war of liberation shall start. Will you behave like a traitor or a patriot?
Kufa	Nobody will prove a greater patriot than me. With my Lomwe recruits from Nsoni, I will fight to the end whatever the end shall be. I will bring with me every medical tool, Treat the wounded in a manner I was taught at the H.H.I. Medical School.
Chilembwe	Good, now the die is cast, Nyasaland shall be set free at last.
Kaduya	But please, Kufa don't change your mind again. Be steadfast, you are a gentleman.
Kufa	Change my mind, that I will not do. I'll fight till the last enemy drops dead And we celebrate our victory with holy wine and bread.
Chilembwe	Let us proceed according to this master plan, Which must be executed from early evening till dawn. Kaduya, you will lead your men from River Mbombwe. Kufa, lead yours from Nsoni and meet Kaduya in Limbe; From there jointly proceed to Mandala ammunition store, Seize the guns, bullets, do nothing more. Send some men to Nyambadwe to deliver a few guns to Njilima. Again a few other weapons send to the men at Midima.

	Both you, Kaduya and Kufa, then bring the rest
	Of the guns here. After a short rest
	We will start the general uprising.
	The struggle for freedom will then be in full swing.
	Wilson Zimba, where are you, dear brother?
Zimba	I am here, Sir.
Chilembwe	Why have you been so silent?
	I thought you were absent.
	You will lead the freedom army tomorrow
	Accompanied by Chimbiya and make raids at Magomero.
	On the Bruce estate the only good white man there is a dead one,
	Go and kill them all starting with Willie Livingstone;
	His servants have heard him say
	'I will kill Chilembwe one day'
	Tomorrow he will be the first,
	To die and bite the dust.
	But do not hurt or touch the women,
	Neither should you kill the children.
	Wanton killing is an abomination.
	God may deny us his blessings if we do not treat the woman and children with compassion.
Kaduya	But Sir, why spare all the white women,
	Some are more cruel than their men?
Chilembwe	It's a command I have received from heaven
	That says spare the women and the children.
Kaduya	Thanks, it's clear now.
	Before you, our leader and God our Creator, I bow.
Chilembwe	Once more to you Zimba, Wilson.
	Are you prepared to lead the battalion.
	And attack the estate condemned as the worst?
Zimba	Great leader, you have given me a job that I will do with zest.
	For sweet revenge I will get at Willie Livingstone.
	After thirteen years of service he dismissed me for no fair reason.

Chilembwe	You, Kuchale, depart right now, For Ntinda village in Ntcheu. Say to the brave Philip Chinyama, Chilembwe says, "seize the *boma*. Then move southwards, cross the Shire river. Come and link with the main battle here."
Kuchale	Pastor, beloved leader, behold I go, I will travel to Ntinda village with the speed of a swallow.
Chilembwe	Matola, you take this letter To Tunduru and give it to the German officer there. In this documents I propose, We join forcers with the Germans and fight a common cause.
Kufa	That sounds odd to me; What good can come out of this alliance? As far as I can see The Germans are white Like the British whom we want to fight. Moreover the Germans are also a colonial power, No less brutal, if you remember How they crushed the Maji Maji revolt. Alliance with the Germans? Reverend, perish the thought
Chilembwe	Have no misgivings about the wisdom Of linking with the Germans to regain our freedom. The United States won independence with the help of French soldiers That previously had been trying to make them French colonial subjects.
Kaduya	What our God-given leader has thought about With utmost care always turns out to be right. To doubt what he decides is treacherous. I wonder, Kufa, are you really with the rest of us?
Kufa	Here I stand and to the battle field I will go, With my own hands to strike imperialism with the biggest blow. I can say no more my action will bear me.

Kaduya	And we will see.
Chilembwe	Now let us pray. *Lord, from this day.* *The struggle against oppression has begun.* *Give us strength till the battle is won.* *In the name of our Spiritual Saviour* *We conclude this prayer.*
All	Amen.

Scene II

Linjesi, Zimba, Chimbiya and twenty others at Linjesi's house – Magomero

Linjesi	Have you finished eating the fish?
Zimba	Yes. It has given us the strength to fight to the finish.
Linjesi	You will find the job easy to do. From Livingstone's room I've removed the bullets and other weapons too. Livingstone does not know this; Tonight it will be death, not his wife that he will kiss.
Zimba	Well done. Which is the best Approach to the house, south, east or west?
Linjesi	The east; they won't see you coming. Walk gently to avoid grass rustling.
Zimba	We'll do as you say, Anything else we must do by the way?
Linjesi	Take with you this cat, Go and throw it at The door. It's going to slip into the house In the way it has done before, hunting a mouse. Livingstone will go and open the door As he has done before To throw the cat out, Then rush in and kill the lout.

Zimba	That idea is ingenious and bright. How did you come to think of it?
Linjesi	I've worked for the Livingstones for many years, I know their habits, strengths and weaknesses.
Zimba	*(Turning to the armed fighters)* We must approach Livingstone's House without the slightest noise. If there is anything wrong with you such as a stuffed throat or nose, Clear it out right now.
All	*(All hem, hem, blowing the nose)*

Scene III

At Livingstone's house, Livingstone, Mrs. Livingstone, Mrs. McDonald, Nyasa, the little girl

Livingstone	Nyasa, my dear daughter, What are you doing there?
Nyasa	Feeding my doll with milk And dressing it in silk.
Livingstone	It's now nine pm, The usual time For you to go to bed.
Nyasa	Not yet daddy. I will wait for mum To come out of the bathroom. She has not yet Kissed me goodnight.
Livingstone	*(Turning to the guest)* Sorry, Mrs. McDonald, I've virtually ignored your presence Trying to put a bit of sense Into the little girl.
Mrs. McDonald	With me all is well.
Livingstone	Did you enjoy your dinner?

Mrs. McDonald	Very much so, thank you. Your boy Hinges is a first class cook and servant too.
Livingstone	Hinges has indeed acquired the skill to cook and bake bread, This is why twice Kitty has dissuaded me from firing the blockhead.
Mrs. McDonald	Why do you want to dismiss such a fine servant?
Livingstone	The bloody native is no longer compliant. Several times I've warned Hinges To stop attending subversive sermons At the so-called church of John Chilembwe Near the River Mbombwe. He has steadily defied my command. In what he does there's something underhand, All this because of John Chilembwe.
Mrs. McDonald	Who is John Chilembwe?
Livingstone	A Native so-called pastor who in the guise of religion Preaches sermons full of sedition.
Mrs. McDonald	Oh, what does he say?
Livingstone	He tells his followers every Sunday That Africa belongs to the African And not to the white man, Chilembwe is a devil incarnate. He has made our estate employees uppital and obstinate. Now I feel I must eliminate that black rat.
Mrs. McDonald	How do you do that?
Livingstone	He likes going into the jungle poaching Game. Next time I see him there as I go hunting I will release a bullet into his swollen head That will at once make him fall dead.
Mrs. McDonald	Won't that be criminal?
Livingstone	Killing a dangerous native is not criminal at all, I must get Chilembwe out of the way And forestall the day

He might bring death upon us.

(Mrs. Livingstone appears at the sitting room in a bathing suit)

Kitty	Willie, there is a cat, Hurry up, throw it out.
Livingstone	But where is Hinges?
Kitty	He has gone back to the boys quarters.
Livingstone	Oh the bloody native, He no longer asks for my permission to knock off.
Mrs. McDonald	Let me hold baby Alistair While you chase after the cat up there.
Livingstone	Thank you *(Hands baby to Mrs. McDonald)* *Gets hold of the cat and opens the door to throw it out* *Chilembwe's men rush in led by Zimba*
Zimba	Don't close the door, man,
Livingstone	*Chiyani, Chiyani*, what do you want you bloody natives all over there?
Zimba	To eat with you your last supper.
Livingstone	Rubbish, clear out.
Zimba	To be more exact We are here to set up a court Of justice and put you on trial For treating any black person like an animal.
Livingstone	What do you take yourself to be?
Zimba	Human beings like yourself, can't you see?
Livingstone	You are mere savages, Bloody fools and knaves.
Chimbiya	Zimba, you are wasting time, Talking – here I am Speaking with my spear. *(stabs Livingstone)*
Livingstone	Oh dear! Kitty, where is the gun, where is the bullet? The savages are attacking me right and left.

Kitty	Oh, you people don't kill my husband, please. You are after his money, I suppose; Here it is, take it and go.
Zimba	Your money, no. We are here to get back our stolen land And bring freedom to our country Nyasaland By killing all bad white men while sparing good men, As well as the women and children.
Kitty	*(Sees Livingstone fall down in the door)* Oh Willie must you die Without even saying goodbye? Here revive by sipping a bit of wine From the best Scottish vine.
Zimba	*(Snatching the bottle)* Don't do that, your husband must die. This is a command from on High. *(Another white man in pyjamas barefooted staggers in)*
McCormack	When I heard natives were attacking my boss Livingstone I threw down My bottle of beer, I left in a hurry to come here. The natives then stabbed me on the back. Pain, the pain, alack- *(collapses)*
Zimba	*(Addressing the white women)* Now ladies, we will treat you as our white sisters. Our God anointed leader has given strict orders Not to hurt you but just take you to our mission, Where David Kaduya will arrange for your deportation. But all bad white men we must kill. After stealing our lands they have called us names contemptible Twenty million fellow Africans all over Africa And ten million fellow blacks in America Are at this very hour fighting to end white man's inhumanity To us blacks. In place there must be universal fraternity. What we have done here at Magomero

Is to sow the seed that will germinate as Africa's freedom tomorrow.
I have spoken enough, white sisters, let's move on
To the Providence Industrial Mission.

Scene IV

At Mandala: Kaduya, Mkulichi, Chimpele and others

Watchman	Who are you people coming up there, Walking suspiciously towards Mandala buildings at this late hour?
Kaduya	Don't raise the alarm, To you we mean no harm,
Watchman	Well then, what is your intention?
Kaduya	From you we seek cooperation. Give us the guns so that Chilembwe may set you and us free.
Watchman	My fellow Blackman, With a broad nose like mine, Can he seize this country from the British? You men are talking rubbish.
Kaduya	Stop insulting our God-given leader, Otherwise we treat you as a traitor.
Watchman	Oh you people just go away, As a good Muslim my masters I will not betray.
Chimpele	Well comrades in the name Of my brother John, let's not waste time Trying to reason with this white man's dog, With the blessings of God Here I go with my knife. *(Stabs the watchman)*
Watchman	*Nkhondo*, Violence, help, they deprive me of my life. War, war, help ho-ho-ho! They kill me for saying no, no, no.

Kaduya	Hurry up, break into the arsenal Before those white people at the Central Sports Club Come to disturb Us from achieving our noble cause Having heard the noise.

Scene V

At the Central Sports Club: Thorburn, Roach, House Servant, Smith, Macfarlane

Thorburn	Well, ladies and gentlemen, Before we start this evening's function Let us stand up and sing God save our gracious King. *(They sing)*
Thorburn	Rule Britannia!
All	Over Africa and India!
Thorburn	Britannia rules the waves of the sea.
All	For a thousand years thus it must be.
Thorburn	Ladies and gentlemen all, Let us remind ourselves, the aim of this jumble sale Is to raise funds to be sent to Belgium For the relief of victims of Kaiser Wilhelm. Here is the silver platter. Who makes the first offer?
Smith	One pound.
Thorburn	One pound, one pound.
McPherson	One pound and ten.
Thorburn	Any other bid?
Robertson	Two. *(A servant breaks in)*
Servant	Bwanas, masters, stop, listen to me, At Mandala, there is a war, go and see.

	I have heard the watchman cry *Nkhondo, nkhondo* Which means war, war, help me, ho, ho, ho.
Roach	Those must be the Germans, What do you think?
Thorburn	No time of thinking let's pick up our guns, Go and repulse the Huns.

Scene V

At PIM: Chilembwe, Morrison, Chigamba, Zimba

Morrison	I hear people singing.
Chilembwe	From which direction is the music coming?
Morrison	Northwards, let me go find out What the singing is all about.
Chigamba	Leave that to me. By the side of our leader you must all the time be. *(After a few minutes Chigamba comes back)*
Chilembwe	Now tell us what you know; Are the singers friendly, yes or no?
Chigamba	They are the people you sent to Magomero. Singing with voices joyful and mellow.
Chilembwe	Let us listen. **Chorus** *Stand up, stand up for freedom,* *Sons of Africa, never mind the doom.* *Stand up for freedom, our God-given right.* *Stick to the sword, liberation is in sight.* *Stand up for Africa, as long as you can.* *It's God who gave Africa to the black man.* *Blessed is Chilembwe our God chosen leader;* *He has summoned us to fight near and far.* *(They arrive in procession)*
Zimba	Great Chilembwe, here we come.

Chilembwe	You are all welcome.
Zimba	God is great, just see. *(Indicating parcel)*
Chilembwe	God has always been great and will ever be. What news have you brought to us? To hear it we are eager and anxious.
Zimba	Wrapped in the sack over there is the skull Of the Magomero Estates Manager, a man dreadful and cruel. I am talking of William Jervis Livingstone. With his *chikoti* he'll flog servants no more for he's as dead as a stone.
Chilembwe	The blood of the tyrant and oppressor, When mixed with that of a patriotic soldier, Waters the tree of freedom, Purifies a republic or kingdom
All	*Mau, Mau* the leader has spoken. Lets sing Alleluia, Amen.
Chilembwe	Is that all you have done?
Zimba	We have also killed McCormick and Ferguson But failed to get at Robertson. His servant held us at bay Meanwhile Robertson and his wife slipped away. Instead we killed his houseboy As he was shouting 'I will do or die!
Chilembwe	Whoever is fighting with them, Has only himself to blame For whatever patriots do to his life. That's the way things go during a bloody strife.
All	*Mau, mau,* the leader has spoken. Let's all sing alleluia, Amen.
Chilembwe	What have you done to the white women And to their children?
Zimba	We have taken them captive,

	They will be arriving here alive. Mrs. Livingstone is dragging her feet, She is shocked and disconsolate.
Chilembwe	With the PIM hammock go and give Mrs. Livingstone a lift. Take to the white ladies some food. Be swift. Don't bring them here. Take them to Chiradzulu Administrative Centre, But first bring me a piece of paper I must write them a letter.

Dear Madams,

At first I ordered that you should be brought to PIM. Now I have decided you should be taken to Chiradzulu Administrative Centre. I have given strict instructions that no white woman or child be killed. Therefore have no fear for your lives. But tell your men we Blacks want Africa back. God gave it to us. Your men have stolen our continent from us. That's why right now twenty million Africans all over the continent have taken up arms to regain their God given heritage.
Africa for the African.

Chilembwe	Wilfred Mtambo, go and deliver this letter.
Ntambo	With pleasure, pastor. *(exits)*
Zimba	By this time, should Kaduya not be back with his men? Surely Blantyre is not as far away as heaven.
Morrison	Perhaps the guns they are bearing amount to a heavy load That slows down their marching on the road.
Zimba	Ah, wait a minute, who is coming up there?
Chimbiya	He is Pilgrim Chigamba Who in a sense resembles you, Zimba.
Chigamba	*(Enters)* As I stood on the ant-hill, I saw my uncle David Kaduya coming; He and his army should soon be arriving.
Chimbiya	Bearing plenty of guns I hope.
Chigamba	Nope.

Zimba	Were they singing As they were marching?
Chigamba	I heard neither tenor nor bass.
Zimba	If so, what sort of news are they bringing to us?
Chilembwe	Don't be anxious. Everything will come our way On this historical day. *(Kaduya arrives, looking sad)*
Zimba	Welcome general Kaduya. Are you bringing us news worthy of a halleluiah?
Kaduya	I love delivering good news, But I also hate telling lies.
Chilembwe	Did anything go wrong, oh God? Go on, let the truth be told.
Kaduya	We called on the Mandala arsenal. Coaxed the watchman. He was not cooperative at all. He raised an alarm, *Nkhondo,* war, ho-ho, So we gave him a deadly blow. Fully armed white men soon arrived. Those of us who could not run fast enough were shot dead.
Chilembwe	Is the brilliant John Gray Kufa among the dead?
Kaduya	Kufa was not with us there. Our men went to his house to search for him. He was nowhere, But his lieutenant Khumbanyiwa did arrive. He too has escaped alive.
Chilembwe	Oh shame on John Gray To lose heart on such a brave day. Where is my brother James?
Kaduya	He's one of those the enemies have killed, alas. They have left his body and those of three others lying On the grounds of the District Office as a warning To other people not to give positive response To the fight for our country's independence.
Chilembwe	Have any of the chiefs brought

	With them their fighting men?
Stephen Mkulichi	The chiefs that I've seen Are seizing our men and handing them to the Security Force.
Chilembwe	Hmm, with only ten guns to share among a thousand of us We are ill-equipped for victory. This much I can say, I feel sorry. Let us admit the uprising has been premature For now give up; we will try again in future.
Kaduya	No great one, we must put In yet another fight. We agreed to strike blow after a blow. With spears, stone and arrows until all the oppressors die or go.
Chilembwe	Stephen, what do you say?
S. Mkulichi	We must continue with the fight day after day.
Chilembwe	Zimba, are you in agreement with that?
Zimba	Certainly, Sir, we must keep on with the fight.
Njilima	The cause is lost.
Kaduya	Oh coward, it's not.
Chilembwe	I easily kindled in you the fire but, I can't as easily put it out. May the fervour for Africa's Freedom keep raging in you, The liberation of mother Africa is a job we must do.
	(Chigamba comes running breathless)
Chigamba	Security Forces are coming there. I have seen them; they are across the river.
Kaduya	They are coming, aha, aha! Let them do so, hurrah, hurrah. There go I to confront the foe, There go I to strike him with the deadly freedom blow.
Zimba	Wherever you go, Kaduya,

	There will I also go, fighting, alleluia.
Chilembwe	With a whip did Jesus not drive out the money changers Who had turned the Jerusalem Holy Temple into a den of thieves and robbers? Give me that gun I must go and take part In driving away the Vandals before they start Desecrating our Holy New Jerusalem Temple.
Kaduya	Oh please, don't say that, Sir, you make my heart tremble. As I imagine what might happen to you our God-given Leader. You are our father, we are your children. If the enemies kill me, someone will take my place and carry on With the struggle; if they kill you, in your place there will be none.
Chilembwe	Give me the gun, I insist. If they kill me, God will provide a substitute.
Zimba	What Kaduya says is right, Sir. Allow us to advise you against your unshakeable will. Instead of coming with us, go to the top of Chilimankwanje Hill. There like Moses wave your wand. It will strengthen our forces; we'll drive out the colonisers of Nyasaland.
Chilembwe	This is not the time to dispute and disagree, To the hill will I go, wave the wand while seated on a tree.
Zimba	Thank you, Sir. Now Morrison accompany the leader there, To the hill of destiny As bodyguard and good company.
Morrison	That certainly will I do. What happens to my uncle must happen to me too.

Scene VI

At Michezime: Chilembwe, S. Mkulichi, Chigamba, Chambo, Kaduya, Chimbiya, Juwa, Mrs. Chilembwe

Chilembwe	(*To Mkulichi*) Tell us the war's progress Now that we are here at Michezime place.
Mkulichi	At first we went and defeated The enemy forces, they retreated. We returned to base singing our victory song, Thinking they would not be back, but we were wrong. The following day, I am sorry to say, Guided by that traitor Lipenga, They attacked us before any of us could reach for his spear or *panga*, Many of us have been killed, Many more have been wounded.
Chilembwe	Heavenly Father, receive the souls of the patriots, we pray thee. Do you want to say something, Willie?
W. Chigamba	With sorrow I report, Sir, That the New Jerusalem Church exists no longer. The enemy forces have turned it into rubble.
Chilembwe	Don't you worry, young one, Time will come when I or someone Else will come and rebuild the holy shrine, And the glory of the Lord will upon our faces once more shine. By the way, I don't see Kaduya among you, By bad luck, is he killed too?
S. Mkulichi	He has just been wounded On the leg, but is not dead.
Chambo	Ah, there comes the brave man leaping, A battle song whistling.
Chilembwe	Sorry, David, you are wounded;

	Pray God that one day through your suffering the black man's freedom will be regained.
Kaduya;	About me don't be troubled in your heart, pastor. When people go to war They know beforehand, They won't all come back healthy and sound. But my real sorrow is that those We have killed among enemy soldiers Are all fellow Africans. I failed to shoot their white commanding officers, Who were using Blacks as their shields.
Chilembwe	That's what they have been doing all along, But eliminating those who behave like Benedict Arnold is not wrong. Blessed are those who face doom For the sake of African freedom. They will be honoured like George Washington In the hour of Africa's dawn. As for you, valiant Chimbiya there, People will say you were their Simon Bolivar.
Chimbiya	*(Spits down)* All your eloquence is just rubbish. You deceived us all that we could drive out the British. See how many of us are killed, some crippled for life, But neither you, nor your wife. The education you got in America Was good only for misleading people in Africa, All that you say is lie, lie, And make us all die, die. You are a leader to darkness, God in heaven is my witness.
Kaduya	How can you say such things against our God given leader? Ask for forgiveness before the Lord strikes you dead right there.
Chimbiya	*(Now looking repentant)* Truly this will count as my day of shame, For like Simon Peter in Jerusalem I've rejected my leader before a crowd.

	Brave and kindly pastor, forgive me for saying things that are beneath a coward.
Chilembwe	That big wound on your leg can make any kind Of person frantic and lose his mind; This much I understand. I've already forgiven you, brave son of Nyasaland.
Chimbiya	Thank you pastor, Now in my heart I feel better.
Chilembwe	Stephen, ask the people to draw nearer, I want to say something before we part from one another,
Mkulichi	Silence, ho, ho, all of you. When I say all of you I mean you too. *(pointing at someone)*
Chilembwe	The war of independence has not gone well. For us to continue fighting would be like descending into hell. It's not due to lack of bravery That we have lost the fight but the treachery Of those in whom we placed out trust As we went out to fight. Truly it has been said in the struggle for freedom and independence, There is always one among the patriots with the impudence And the greed for money to play Judas Iscariot. In the American struggles for independence Benedict Arnold was the idiot. But take heart we have only lost a battle. One day, better equipped we will continue the struggle. After the darkest night The sun rises, shines with all its might. Truly, I say to you, sisters and brethren, There are among you who will live to see Africa's glorious dawn. The Lord hears us as we sing Enoch Sontonga's song, Lord bless Africa. We too will one day erect the Statute of Liberty like that of America.

	For now I charge you, Isaac Chambo,
	To lead our women and children via Mkombezi *dambo*
	With this white flag held high.
	Go and meet the British Commander,
	Government soldiers and say, it's better
	For our women and children to live than to die.
Chambo	Of all people, you have chosen me, why?
Chilembwe	Because you have not held a leading position
	In planning this war of liberation.
	The white commander is likely
	To punish you rather lightly.
Juwa	Do you want Chambo to hand us to the white commander?
	Are you not exposing us to greater danger?
	Why not take us to one of our chiefs?
Chilembwe	Chiefs are going to treat you worse than the white people.
	Those royal cowards want to demonstrate that about what we have done they had no prior knowledge at all.
	To absolve themselves
	From suspicion they are already hunting us with the zeal of hungry wolves.
	As for the whites, we have done no harm to their women,
	Neither have we killed their children,
	They are human enough to reciprocate kindness
	To the tender and harmless.
Juwa	But where are you yourself going?
Chilembwe	I'll try to find my way back to America
	To see Dr Dubois who leads the Congress of Africa,
	And suggest we link our fighting forces,
	Continue the struggle no matter how long it lasts.
John Chilembwe Junior	I'll go with you, Daddy.
Chilembwe	No, stay with mum and Donald.
Ida Chilembwe	The child is right, don't say no.
	Wherever you go, we must also go.

	We have always lived together as one, Father, Mother and Children.
Chilembwe	Ida, my wife, You have always been to me as dear as my own life, To part from you and the children Is not easy, but now this must be done.
Ida	No woman has a better husband than I have. From you flows abundant love To me and our dear children. This is why I say, don't leave us alone. Whatever happens to you Let it happen to us too.
Chilembwe	A loving family man Spares his wife and children The risks that accompany him As he struggles against a foreign regime. Before I take the ship to America I'll trudge through the forests of Africa, Encountering snakes, leopards and lions, The jungle is full of thistles and scorpions. Must you and our beloved children share with me such a dangerous life? No, Ida, my dear wife Since our wedding day I have never insisted that you should obey me, But now it is different as you can see.
Ida	Your decision is always the best. Before you depart won't you pray for us and the rest?
Chilembwe	That I must do, For Nyasaland and Africa too. *(Prays) God our Father there in heaven,* *We Africa's children* *Thank you for the gift of a continent* *Vast, fertile, everything abundant.* *We thank thee for the rivers big and small, the Shire, the Congo and the Nile up there,* *For the Zambezi, the Ruvuma, the Niger,*

| | We thank thee for the Nyasa;
We thank you for the Nyanza,
Yet we do not enjoy these great gifts.
Your other children have stolen them from us.
Heavenly father, send to Africa courageous men as soon
    as possible
To make Africa free and indomitable.
Alleluia. |
|---|---|
| **All** | Amen |
| **Chilembwe** | Till we meet again, God be with you. |
| **All** | And you too.
(They depart) |

Scene VII

At Mombezi, meeting the army

Chambo, Juwa, Mrs. Chilembwe, Capt Triscott, Thorburn, Roach

| **Chambo** | Having walked more than a mile
Let's sit down for a while.
Rest is good for elderly women
And also the toddling children. |
|---|---|
| **Mai Juwa** | That's kind of you.
But, Chambo, you ought to have referred to me too.
Though I am not old, within me,
As you can see,
I carry a baby that soon
Will be born. |
| **Chambo** | Indeed you too deserve a good rest,
So that out of you we may hope for the best. |
| **Mrs. Chilembwe** | We are talking of resting
But look where the soldiers are coming. |
| **Mai Juwa** | Oh' mother! They are armed to their teeth,
Looking as frightful as death. |

All Women	Woe is us today! When they arrive here what shall we say?
Mai Juwa	Your husband, Ida, has put us into trouble. Why did he provoke white people? And why did you not reason him out of a scheme so foolish? Now see all of us are going to perish.
Mrs. Chilembwe	He did not confide in me What he was planning to do or be. To me also the revolt is a surprise. I admit my husband has done something unwise.
Mai Juwa	Men make a great mistake By not inviting women to partake Of public affairs. They simply accuse us of gossiping But is gossiping as evil as fighting?
Chambo	Ladies this is not the time for grumbling. Stand up, start walking Towards the security forces *(Addressing the white soldiers)* Bwanas, peace, oh please peace; With this white flag raised high We sue for peace, to war we say goodbye. Here is a letter from our leader. He sent me to surrender to you these fifty women And these twenty five children.
Capt. Triscott	*(Reading Chilembwe's letter)* The bearer of this letter is Isaac Chambo. He took no part in planning the up-rising, He has taken no part in fighting. This is the reason I have sent him to escort our women and children. As we have treated your women and children kindly, so I appeal To you to do the same to our women and children.
Capt. Triscott;	Where is Chilembwe himself?
Chambo	That I don't know.

Capt. Triscott	Stupid answer! Bind this man to that tree. *(The soldiers bind Chambo)* Now tell me, where is he? If you don't I'll shoot you, The women and children too.
Chambo	Sir, ask his wife, Spare my life.
Capt. Triscott	Are you Chilembwe's female
Mrs. Chilembwe	He calls me his lady wife.
Capt. Triscott	You, a lady wife, don't be silly, That honour is reserved for white women only. Though you are a half caste You are nearer black than white, Hence not a lady but female native. To call you a lady would be naïve. Do you understand?
Mrs. Chilembwe	Yes, Sir.
Capt. Triscott	Now, then where is your husband?
Mrs. Chilembwe	We parted from him at Michezime station, He went towards Mulanje mountain.
Capt. Triscott	Did he say where he was going?
Mrs. Chilembwe	He said he and Morrison were going to America To recruit Negroes for the liberation of Africa.
Capt. Triscott	Thorburn and Roach; take these women captives To Zomba while the rest of us pursue the fugitives

Scene VIII

At Magomero: Bruce, Thorburn, Ida, D. Kaduya, Linjesi, Roach, Gulugufe, Sixpence, Namakwa, M'maniwa

Thorburn	Mr. Bruce, good afternoon.
Bruce	Good afternoon, Mr. Thorburn.

Thorburn	I understand you were with the army at Karonga When the tragedies took place.
Bruce	Yes I arrived here at dawn Dog-tired and worn.
Thorburn	Do you suspect any accomplice Of the murder to whom we may administer summary justice?
Bruce	I suspect this native servant of the Livingstones. His name is Hinges. I heard Willie Livingstone say more than once that he did not trust the rascal, But Mrs. Livingstone objected to the boy's dismissal.
Mrs. Livingstone	Because of his capable hands I was made to believe He was an honest and loyal native. Now I feel sure he is the one who stole the bullets from our bedroom. Thereby ensuring my husband's doom.
Bruce	Where were you, Hinges, When your master was being attacked by the savages?
Linjesi	I was at home sleeping, Totally unaware of what was happening.
Mrs. Livingstone	You lie, It's you who arranged for my husband to die.
Linjesi	Before God I swear, I am innocent of my master's murder.
Bruce	You guided the insurgents, This other native here is my informant and witness. Come forward Sixpence and say what you know.
Sixpence	I'll speak of what with my own eyes I saw. In the evening of the murders there arrived queer people At the house of Linjesi. One carried an axle, Three carried spears. They were at his house For a short time, then I saw them Going in the direction of Mr. Livingstone's house.

	I thought hey were just going to pass By, but then soon I heard they had killed Mr. Livingstone And taken away the white women.
Linjesi	Sixpence is bearing false witness Against me because one day I snatched from him a pretty girl called Loveness.
Thorburn	*(Pointing at Mrs. Chilembwe)* Did you ever see Hinges at your home Conspiring with your husband?
Mrs. Chilembwe	Many times
Mrs. Livingstone	Hinges, what grievance did you have against us?
Linjesi	Mr. Livingstone now and again flogged me with a *chikoti*.
Thorburn	He has indirectly admitted his role in the conspiracy. He was the main accomplice. Let's not waste time, But get on and execute him. One, two, three, fire.
Roach	Shoot the nigger! *(Several soldiers shoot Linjesi)*
Thorburn	This other boy was a particularly nasty one. Do you recall him, Mrs. Livingstone?
Mrs. Livingstone	Not at all.
Thorburn	He often made your husband lose patience Because of his unbearable impertinence. Willie often flogged him with a *chikoti*
Mrs. Livingstone	Oh no my husband never flogged the natives. His kindness was such that he would assist a lame dog walk over stiles.
Thorburn	What about you, Chilembwe's female. Do you remember anything about him?
Mrs. Chilembwe	He was a frequent visitor at the PIM.
Thorburn	Did he take part in the plot?

Mrs. Chilembwe	Quite a lot
M'maniwa	About me she is telling you lies, Don't believe what she says.
Thorburn	Chilembwe's wife does not lie. You are guilty of the murder, you too must die. One, two, three-fire.
Roach	Shoot the nigger!
Thorburn	Let's proceed to Zomba
Chief Gulugufe	*(Coming at a distance)* Bwanas, don't disperse as yet. Here I bring to you the biggest fish from the net. This is David Kaduya, Chilembwe's next in command. He used to advocate that all white people be killed or expelled from Nyasaland.
Bruce	Who is that native Bringing such a wanted fugitive?
Thorburn	His name is Gulugufe the most cooperative of the chiefs on the Shire Highlands. He has already rounded up many of the insurgents, Though none so much wanted as the one he is bringing now.
Thorburn	*(Facing Mrs. Chilembwe)* Do you recognise this man?
Mrs. Chilembwe	He is David Kaduya.
Thorburn	Did he take part in the plot?
Mrs. Chilembwe	Oh yes, he did quite a lot To incite other natives against white people, He advocated acts most horrible. Such as killing the white women And not sparing even their children.
Thorburn	Do you plead guilty to the charges?
Kaduya	She has mixed truth with lies. This much I admit, I was number two to John Chilembwe

	While masterminding freedom forces by the River Mbombwe.
Bruce	Tell me, native, why did you conspire To kill the whites? Mr. Livingstone was a good overseer. He treated workers and tenants with fairness.
Kaduya	Bruce, don't talk rubbish. All your managers treated Africans with harshness. They brutalised the workers to please you. If I had a gun I should have shot you too.
Bruce	But I have been nice to all employees and tenants. They all have been happier here than anywhere else.
Kaduya	You sent to Njuli that man Roach To seize indigenous people's gardens, and reproach Them as well. You used your white staff To oppress the blacks on your behalf.
Thorburn	Bruce, no more verbal wrangle With this unrepentant criminal who has caused us so much trouble. Here I go. One, two, three, fire.
Roach	Shoot the nigger!
Chief Gulugufe	We found Kaduya at this man's house. They were eating rice.
Namakwa	But I am not a conspirator, Before God I swear.
Thorburn	Ida, did you ever see this man engaged with your husband in the plot?
Mrs. Chilembwe	He used to come and take part.
Namakwa	She is telling a lie Just to make me die.
Thorburn	One, two, three. Fire.
Roach	Shoot the nigger!
Thorburn	With the rest of the captives let's proceed to Zomba.

Scene IX

At Zomba: Mrs. Chilembwe, Zimba, Majawa, Bradbury, Njilima, Thorburn, Judge, Hollis and Mrs. Hollis,

Thorburn	This native female is Chilembwe's wife. She is the key witness.
Judge	Ida, are you a Christian?
Mrs. Chilembwe	Yes, I am a Christian.
Judges	Swear on the Bible that you will say nothing but the truth.
Mrs. Chilembwe	I swear on this Holy Book That I will say nothing but the truth, So help me, oh God.
Thorburn	This man Duncan Njilima, Did he plot with your husband?
Mrs. Chilembwe	Yes he did.
Thorburn	Publicly he must hang till he is dead. This man John Gray Kufa was he with your husband plotting?
Mrs. Chilembwe	He was very active in so doing.
Thorburn	Among this group, Ida, Pick out those who came plotting.
Mrs. Chilembwe	This one there, and this one here. That one here and that one.
Zimba	You shut up your mouth of lies, Mrs. Chilembwe.
Thorburn	You have no right to stop her giving evidence.
Zimba	You white people, what you are doing here is injustice Against innocent people you bear malice. Why in the first instance do you keep our women in jail Forcing them to break stones for a scanty meal? When we took your women captives we treated them with respect, But you treat ours with contempt.

	Send our women back home.
	They have not done, and will not do you any harm.
Thorburn	They are here to testify what they know.
Zimba	No woman took part in our meetings,
	We met in secret all the evenings.
	What Chilembwe's wife has told you are lies,
	She was never with us any of the days
	We met. Through her loose mouth
	She has betrayed innocent men to death.
	For using her mouth to lie
	God will not give her long life here on earth.
	The Angel of Freedom will send her into perdition after her early death.
Thorburn	Alright, indicate your fellow insurgents among these people
	And mention those still in hiding.
Zimba	That I will not do.
	Its up to everyone who took part
	In the planning to say this or that.
Thorburn	The sooner you cooperate in giving evidence
	Against your fellow insurgents,
	The sooner will I let the female captives go.
	Otherwise to your request for their release I say no.
Mrs. Hollis	Why should you do that?
	To force someone bear witness against a friend is unjust.
	Let the African women go.
	Why do you keep on saving no, no?
	British justice must not just be seen,
	It must be seen and done.
Thorburn	Go away, you inferior white woman.
Judge	Prosecutor, bring another accused.
Thorburn	Ida, did you see this man with your husband,
	Plotting to kill white people of Nyasaland?
Mrs. Chilembwe	Yes I saw him many times plotting.
Majawa	She is telling a lie,

	She just wants me to die.
	I have recently arrived from Salisbury
	With my master, Mr. Bradbury
Bradbury	I arrived from Salisbury last week
	With this native, John Majawa, my cook.
	He is a native of this country.
	For the last ten years he has been with me in Rhodesia working diligently,
	Soon after we arrived here three days ago he asked for permission to go and see his relative Sam Bombay.
	A day later news reached me that my cook had been arrested and taken to Zomba.
	In the name of God the Almighty,
	I testify that this native has been arrested through mistaken identity.
Thorburn	My Lord, evidence given by an Englishman
	Is always more reliable than that given by a black person.
	I therefore withdraw the charges against John Majawa.
	He has been mistaken for someone with a similar name who dwells at Namiwawa.
Judge	John Majawa, I acquit you,
	Convinced that with the insurgency you had nothing to do.
Thorburn	This man is Wycliff Chigamba,
	Who like Wilfred Mtambo and Donald Gomba,
	Who you have tried already, took part in the up-rising
	And deserves a death sentence by public hanging.
Judge	Do you have any reason
	Why you should not be given the maximum sentence for high treason?
Chigamba	I was forced to join in the up-rising by my elders.
	I worked as a mere messenger, delivering letters,
	I could not refuse because of fear for my life.
	At one time when I said no, someone nearly stabbed me with a knife.
Judge	How old are you?
Chigamba	I am not old but young.

Judge	When were you born?
Chigamba	Fifteen years ago.
Judge	As you look a mere youth Speaking plausible truth, I give you a lighter sentence. You will be in jail for five years hoping you come out with more sense.
Judge	Accused Khumbanyiwa, do you have anything to say that could be Accepted as mitigation?
Khumbanyiwa	Blame the frustrations I first experienced at Namuli, My original home, then at Namiwawa and Njuli. Shortly after the Resident had fined O'Brien only twenty shillings For killing my daughter, a stranger visited me. His name was David Kaduya. He said "God has sent to us black people our own Messiah, His name is John Chilembwe. He operates his Mission east of the River Mbombwe. He is going to declare Nyasaland independent Of the White rulers and set up black people's own government. Only under such a government can Africans be free." Without much thinking I did agree When he said come and join the revolt. Because of the injustice I had suffered I went and joined in the fight. Frustrations in my life had prevented me to see That Kaduya was misleading me. But though I carried a weapon, I killed no one, African or European. To the truth of what I have said Heaven is my witness, From you, my Lord, I ask for forgiveness.
Judge	Obviously you are but a simpleton. If the white men suddenly abandoned Africa This dark continent would become a replica Of its pre-colonial image.

Everywhere all sorts of evils would rage.
Nothing good existed in Africa until the white man accepted from God the burden
Of civilising the savage and converting the heathen.
Once white men quit, African life here will be nasty, brutal and short.
Tribe will be fighting another tribe, the benefits of civilisation brought by the white man will be lost.
The slave trader will be back,
Light will go, all around will be dark.
Casualties of civil wars will lie unburied here and there.
Much to the pleasure of the maggot and the vulture.
Cannibalism, incest, treachery will reign supreme,
No one will be smiling, everyone will look grim.
However this is just my *obiter dicta*, something said by the way.
I have taken into account what you say.
Instead of capital punishment
I sentence you to ten years imprisonment.

Khumbanyiwa That's indeed better.
Thank you, Sir.

Judge Wilson Zimba, you are found guilty
Of taking part in the up-rising against His Majesty
The King and killing an innocent man, William Jervis Livingstone.
The crimes you have committed are a compound of murder and treason.
Before I pronounce the sentence, do you have any reason for mitigation?

Zimba I see nothing but mockery in that question.
When a person with his foot treads on a snake,
And the snake turns round and hits back,
Who is at fault?
Who should plead the guilt?

Judge Prisoner, Wilson Zimba,
I sentence you to death by public hanging at Bwaila in Zomba.
May the Lord have mercy upon your soul.

Zimba	And may the Lord punish all Who keep other people in subjection. After death they deserve perdition. *(Looking in the direction of Bwaila)* John Gray Kufa, Duncan Njilima, here I come to join you on the Golgotha. Our blood will be spilt together to wash away the *thangata*.
Mrs. Hollis	Prosecutor, you have already been responsible for condemning to public hanging fifty black men, All these for the murder of three white men. The Lord in heaven will punish You for these trials; they are ungodly and unBritish.
Prosecutor	We will hang up to three hundred of them, If they all took part in the crime.
Mrs. Hollis	Why?
Prosecutor	The life of one white man Is equal to that of one hundred black men.
Mrs. Hollis	That's not true at all. God created all human races as equal.
Prosecutor	We have to display our strength So as to preserve the British Empire from untimely death.
Mrs. Hollis	Not all the people you have hanged deserved a death sentence. Some of them you have condemned on scant evidence. British justice has been seen But not done.
Roach	People like you who harbour silly sentiments for the natives are a danger To the continued existence of the British Empire.
Mrs. Hollis	It's those of you who are filled with malice Towards the African and do him injustice That hasten the fall of the British Empire By forcing the native to rebellion due to despair.
Thorburn	Hey, prosecutor and you Roach, Why do you reproach

	Yourselves by talking to this woman and her husband, The most inferior whites whoever came to Nyasaland? Police, where are you? Come, Arrest and deport them.
Mrs. Hollis	Back home we shall go, But this much you must know: By doing the natives wrong You do not help the empire to last long.
Thorburn	Rubbish! You are unfit to be called British.
Mrs. Hollis	Okay, but hark how the condemned sing and pray as they ascend the scaffold. Surely their prayers reach the ears of Almighty God.

Chorus
Stand up, stand up for Africa's freedom,
Sons and daughters of Africa, whatever the doom,
The morning star has risen.
The cock is crowing, heralding Africa's dawn.
Stand up and sing with Enoch Sontonga,
Say and pray in Xhosa, Nyanja, and Tonga:
Nkosi Sikelei Africa, Lord bless Africa,
Lord bless all who die for Africa.
Let's stand up and sing even as they hang us upon the tree,
Rejoice as martyrs. Your blood will set Africa free.
John Chilembwe is on the way to America
From where he will return with Dr Dubois and other friends of Africa.
Alleluia, Amen,
On earth and in heaven.

Scene X: Chilembwe's Last Day

At the house of Flora Nalikata: Chilembwe, Flora Nalikata, two of Nalikata's children, Garnet Kaduya

Garnet Kaduya	Have you seen them Pass by, Chilembwe and other members of the PIM?
Flora Nalikata	I have not seen strangers passing by today, Not even yesterday or the day before yesterday.
Garnet Kaduya	If today or tomorrow you see Strange men, send message to me. The government has put a reward On Chilembwe to be brought alive or dead.
Flora Nalikata	How does Chilembwe look?
Garnet Kaduya	He is slim, dusky and short. He was last seen wearing a blue coat.
Flora Nalikata	Should I see such a man I will let you know.
Garnet Kaduya	Please do so. To me the news will be as sweet as honey. It will give me a chance to earn a lot of money; This money I will share it with you And your two children too. Stay well.
Flora Nalikata	Go well. *(She goes back into the house where Chilembwe and Morrison are hiding)*
Chilembwe	I heard you talking to yet another man.
Flora Nalikata	Yes, and he had a gun.
Chilembwe	From his voice I could tell It was Garnet Kaduya whom I know well As a white man's hungry wolf, Who for the sake of the white man's money wants to deprive me of my life. *(Turning to Morrison)* Morrison, son of my brother, It's now better That we quit this hiding place, Otherwise for nothing we endanger our hostess.
Flora Nalikata	Not for nothing, Sir, but a worthy cause. I am one of the harassed widows. My husband was killed two months ago

	At Karonga, fighting in a white man's war whose purpose I do not know.
	Pastor, you are the guardian of us, the wretched ones of the earth.
	For sheltering you I would not mind risking imprisonment or death.
Chilembwe	God bless you, Flora Nalikata MacDonald, for having looked after us so well.
	Now Morrison, let's depart for Mozambique via Bangala Hill.
Flora Nalikata	I suggest you leave this house dressed in a *chilundu* and *duku* turban,
	In this way each of you will look like a woman.
Chilembwe	Thank you for the clever suggestion, oh, Flora Nalikata MacDonald.
Flora Nalikata	Why do you call me MacDonald?
	It's not my surname.
Chilembwe	You remind me of Flora MacDonald
	Who sheltered Prince Charles Edward
	Of Scotland in the year seventeen forty-five
	From the English invaders who wanted him dead, not alive.
	Madam, for your kindness and patriotism may God bless you.
Flora Nalikata	And you too.
Chilembwe	Stay well.
Flora Nalikata	Reach well.

Scene XII

Garnet Kaduya, Capt. Triscott, Vassal

Capt. Triscott	Now Garnet, our loyal native,
	What progress have you made trailing Chilembwe the fugitive?
Garnet Kaduya	Though I have not yet captured him I hope soon to do so,

	Accompanied as I will be with Kambalame and Naluso.
Triscott	Are you sure?
Garnet Kaduya	Very sure, Sir. For it's now certain Chilembwe is still Within Mulanje District heading for Bangala Hill. One of my informants saw what at first looked like two women Enter the forest accompanied by two children. There in the forest they took off clothes, Handed them to the children. Now in male dress, My informant recognised them as Chilembwe and his nephew Morrison. They looked haggard and forlorn.
Triscott	Good, most loyal native. Go and get Chilembwe dead or alive.
Garnet Kaduya	That certainly will I do, With zeal and zest too. *(Exit Garnet Kaduya, Mandanda, Naluso, Kambalame)*
Vassal	I feel like joining in the hunt.
Triscott	Oh, don't. For a white man the forest is too thick To travel through. Why risk Being shot. If Garnet and the Native police Kill or capture Chilembwe, it is we who shall be mentioned in dispatches to the Colonial Office, After which there might be a promotion, And a decoration.

Scene XIII

Chilembwe, Morrison, Kaduya, Mandanda, Naluso, Kambalame and Useni

Naluso	We have traversed stream after stream that flows to the river Migowi until it's dark. Catching up with Chilembwe is proving to be hard work.

Mandanda	Perhaps he has already entered Mozambique.
Garnet Kaduya	Ah, wait a minute, don't be pessimistic, For behold, what do I see There sitting below that big tree? Surely that is Chilembwe with his brother's son.
Mandanda	There goes the bullet from my gun, Both men are now running away though I have wounded one of them.
Kambalame	Let me shoot the same man and finish him. Down he has fallen but Chilembwe has fled away. *(They approach the dead body)* Who is this man by the way?
Garnet Kaduya	This is Morrison, son of Chimpele, Chilembwe's brother, Though Chilembwe himself has escaped, don't bother. Now that he is alone in this thick forest And we are a team of eight It won't be long before we deliver the fugitive To the Resident, dead or alive.
Naluso	Ah, look there, he's no longer running away but standing still. Perhaps he has lost the will To live. My bullet has shot him in the stomach, But he has not fallen on his back.
Sergeant Useni	I too have shot him but he has not fallen down at all. He must have inoculated himself with magic potion that turns a bullet into a soft ball.
Chilembwe	Countrymen, don't kill me. Instead take me to your white masters to hang me on a tree After I have told them the truth That whatever they do to me, we Africans are bound to be free.
Mandanda	Chilembwe, what you say proves you to be an idiot. We won't do what you suggest.
Chilembwe	Truly has it been said that the greatest enemy of the freedom fighter

	Is the slave whom the fighter wants to emancipate from the slave master. And here you are, my own people, you have come to kill me. Instead of leaving me to go scot-free.
Garnet Kaduya	I have no time for your politics, Chilembwe, it's full of tricks. My profession is to use the gun Against those who commit treason. Now as you stand there my bullet will hit you in the head, Aha, at last he has fallen down reeling; he will soon stop dead.
Chilembwe	*(His hand raised)* Lord my God, let my doo-oo-m Be the beginning of Africa's free-do-m. *(Dies)*
Garnet Kaduya	Let's search his pockets, perhaps there Is money for us to share.
Mandanda	In this pocket I have found fifteen pounds. In this other only 0,303 cartridges. In his hand he just carried the Bible But no rifle.
Naluso	Truly this man was a dandy, see how he's dressed. Here a neat blue coat, There a coloured shirt and a striped pyjama, Grey flannel trousers seldom worn by anyone at the *boma*.
Mandanda	Hey, look at this burn of recent date On the left side of his left foot. His body is emaciated and bony.
Naluso	He must have suffered a good deal of agony.
Garnet Kaduya	Let's not waste time talking about trifles, There may still be Chilembwe's men around bearing rifles. Make a pole and rope hammock While I cycle to Mulanje *boma* and knock At the door of the Resident, The jolly good man Colin Grant,

To herald
The good news that Chilembwe is dead.
When you arrive with Chilembwe's corpse on the hammock
And on the Resident's door knock,
You will find the prize money waiting for you
And of course for me too.
(After walking away a while, Garnet Kaduya comes back)
And last word for each and everyone of us.
Let's not go about boasting that we are the ones who killed this
Man. We would be exposing our lives to danger.
Chilembwe's uncaptured followers are still hiding here and there.
Instead we should encourage rumours that he turned into a bird
And flew back to America via Scotland. Agreed?

All   Yes, indeed.

www.ingramcontent.com/pod-product-compliance
Lightning Source LLC
Chambersburg PA
CBHW011746220426
43667CB00019B/2918